Copyright © 2011 Juana Wooldridge

All rights reserved. Printed and bound in the United States of America. No part of this book may be reproduced or transmitted in any form or by any means, electronic or mechanical, including photocopying, recording, or by any information storage or retrieval system except by a reviewer who may quote brief pages in a review to be printed in a magazine or newspaper, without written permission from the publisher and the author:

Published by 220 Publishing
(A Division of 220 Communications)
PO Box 8186
Chicago, IL 60680-8186
www.220communications.com
www.twitter.com/220publishing

220 Communications
Printed in the United States of America

ISBN: 978-1-4507-6989-1

Cover design and Inside Illustration by Julie M. Holloway
www.jmhartstudio.com
www.twitter.com/jmhartstudio
www.facebook.com/jmhartstudio
+1 815.582.7234

"There are days when I am really low or worried about a situation.

Then I turn on my computer, and there is Juana, taking my hand, reversing the negativity, shocking me back to reality, putting things in the proper perspective, making my day. Thank you so much for your insight, for your spirituality, and for being YOU!"

Jessie McBee-Bridges, Chicago, IL

Contents

I GIVE THANKS   .10.

MY DEDICATION .12.

REFLECTIONS:

INSPIRATIONAL .14.

TRIALS MAKE US STRONGER .27.

OVERCOMING DEPRESSION .38.

FORGIVENESS .43.

SELF-ESTEEM .48.

KNOW HOW TO BE ALONE .57.

BEAUTY .61.

LOVE .65.

GIVING .78.

RELIGION .81.

FRIENDSHIP .95.

SEXY .98.

POETRY TO MY LOVE .104.

MY SPIRIT .117.

ABOUT THE AUTHOR - BIO .133.

   Juana Wooldridge

ABOUT THE EDITOR - Bio .135.

   Leslie Gordon

Intro:

This book takes you on a journey of my writing, which is how I found myself again. I was lost; I didn't know how to connect with God anymore. I didn't know who I was. My writing brought me back. I started writing and people responded to it, and daily followed me through my coming back. I wrote about love, heartache, trials, and much more. My poetry became the favorite of many as well. You can follow me on my spiritual journey and find clarity in your own being.

I became a voice of inspiration to others. I am celebrating the gift I've been given to write. I reflect and look back on daily having the privilege to share my heart with others, to share my imperfections and my beauty, most of all to share the wisdom that God has given me. God's favor is the best thing in the world. God has walked with me because I took delight in him, he has spiritually talked me through all things. I realize that I can't be praised for something God has done and God did this work in me and through me. This is my purpose. You will notice that the book is divided into sections so that you can go to the section you feel like reading and be inspired!

My heart and soul are filled and overflowing with love and passion for life. I step out with love and that makes fear surrender to me. Anxiety and worry have raised their white flag. Honey, the sweetness of life protects me in its thickness and pureness. I have risen in strength and insight. I have arrived at the door of understanding and it has opened to me. My heart is colored in the wonders of life. The strength of my fire surrounds me and consumes me. I taste every moment, I feel everything with intensity. I have peace that calms me and grabs hold of me to give me rest. I am calm in my passion. Yes, a fire with purpose, I am. I am complete at this moment with all that I need. God is everywhere and certainly I am complete in God's love. I am receiving all things, I lack nothing. There is no advantage over me, I am strong. I walk in the power I have been given.

"Juana Wooldridge has lit a spark in the minds of her growing audience of readers; provoking deep thinking about issues of love, God, religion, relationships, parenthood, friendship, sports, and a wide range of other topics of interest. It's time for a broader audience to experience her, and get the benefit of her encouragement and seeds of self-introspection. Poetic and inspiring, she reminds us of the beauty of life, the possibilities of the spirit, and the inner untapped potential that lies dormant in each of us."

~Lester McCarroll Jr.

I GIVE THANKS

I give thanks first and foremost to God for everything in my life. I am thankful that when I was so lost and in need, God did not abandon me. I owe my life and all the wonderful blessings in it to my relationship with God. My search in life to be closer to God, to find myself, and to find peace led me to writing this book. Since I was very young, I would pray in my bed every night and have conversations with God. I would pour out my heart, my love, my fea, and my tears. God heard me and answered my cry for help. The relationship I developed with God through those nights filled with prayer molded my heart to love deeply and cling to wisdom. Faith has moved mountains in my life because I know God is with me and protects me. I have been blessed for being attentive to God. God is my greatest treasure and friend.

I also want to thank my family and friends for their loving support. I cannot mention everyone so I want you all to know that I love you very much. I want to thank my son Blace for bringing me joy, growth and an even greater reason to be the best version of myself. My son inspires me and enlightens me with the purity of his soul. Children are precious. I want to give a special thanks to my father for his friendship and his loving support. Growing closer to my father has helped me tremendously. I feel more loved and secure as a result. He has helped me make a new life away from the community of my youth. I needed a way out and God provided my father as that way. He took it as his responsibility to watch after Blace and me; he wanted me to get free. He helped me so that I could break out of the prison of depression that I was in, and now I am so happy. I want to thank my mother for loving my son and for helping me care for him. Even though we don't have a relationship anymore, I know she loves me very much and she is able to pour that into my son. Being away from my son in order to work has been emotionally hard on me. I've cried many nights but I know my son has had me there with him all the time because of my mother. My mother and I have this way of loving wholeheartedly and my son is showered with our love. I want to thank my Facebook family and my friends. I've grown into this strong and powerful being because I've been able to walk in God's love and that of others. My friends made me special, the way they love me makes me favored and gifted. So thank all of you for making me special. The love that I have been watered with has made me blossom into a new and better person. I have thousands of people that have followed my writing for over two years now. I have written faithfully on a daily basis and I have been rewarded with daily heartfelt comments from those that have embraced me and taken me into their homes. Thank you.

Love,

Juana

"You were made on purpose for a great and wonderful purpose."

MY DEDICATION

I dedicate this book to my great aunt, the late Abbey Lincoln. I always had a good and special relationship with her. I lived with her for a short time in my childhood and was with her when she wrote "Throw It Away." Her death was—and still

is—hard for me. Growing up, my grandfather always told me I reminded him of her. I wish she could see me really pursuing the arts and my dreams now. My favorite movie that she starred in was For the Love of Ivy, with Sidney Poitier.

I used to call her and read the Bible to her, or just talk about things in her life and mine. She just poured out wisdom. She would say something so profound, and then say something so innocent and childlike. Her laugh is memorable, as is her career. She was a beautiful woman in every way. I celebrate her music, her love and her wisdom. She was a big part of my growth, and she still is.

The Most Profound Moment of My Life:

The most profound moment of my life was when I stopped needing proof that God exists. I grew up very religious, learning about God. I am thankful for my upbringing because we all need a base to develop spirituality, and I had a wonderful base. I knew all the rules, what I should do and what I shouldn't do. I went to many religious meetings, read the Bible daily and talked about spiritual things. My life was surrounded by God. In the midst of all this, I used to pray to God to give me a sign that he existed.

I remember praying constantly in my youth and asking God to take me to heaven to visit for a bit. I remember asking God to make my light switch go on or off just so I could see it. I wanted proof that God existed, although I believed in God. I think a lot of this stemmed from my desire to get concrete answers from God. I wanted to know why God allowed there to be so many religions. I thought God had to know that this was very confusing. I also knew that people mostly believed in the religion they were taught. I wanted to figure out death. I knew that whenever I died, I wanted a guarantee of what was going to happen to me. I wanted to know why things had to be the way they were. I wanted answers.

As I grew, I went through different stages of spiritual growth. There was a time when it was all about rules. I just wanted to follow the rules and be a good person. I gradually got to this place of recognition of God in me, in my thoughts, and a part of me. I started to realize that seeing myself, or seeing another human being, was seeing God. This was proof that God existed. I started to realize that a flower spoke to me about God, a tree spoke to me about God, and everything did. I was given an inner peace that God was all powerful and I could see in His creation, that God is love. I trusted that in all my questions, the answer was love. This spiritual stage of growth brought me peace.

I took my answer and I became my answer. I tried daily to be love and found that this made me stop needing proof of God's existence. This was so profound because it changed my approach to life. I became more confident and more understanding. I stopped needing things to be right. I started enjoying my life and not judging myself so much. I stopped examining my every move. Becoming love is what I strive for daily and this gives me great peace.

INSPIRATIONAL

"I SEE YOUR BEAUTY! BE STRONG AND BELIEVE IN YOURSELF! DO YOU KNOW WHAT IT TOOK FOR YOU TO GET HERE? A MIRACLE. YOU'RE A MIRACLE. WALK IN YOUR POWER AND THE GREATEST POWER IS IN KNOWING YOUR VALUE. DON'T GIVE UP OR BE AFRAID. YOU CAN DO SO MUCH MORE THAN YOU KNOW. I WANT YOU TO KNOW THAT SO THAT NO ONE CAN TRICK YOU INTO BELIEVING YOU DON'T HAVE WHAT IT TAKES. YOU HAVE WHAT IT TAKES. YOU ALWAYS DID!"

The glass is half full. Have faith and patience. Faith can move mountains, but until the mountain moves, start climbing it. While you're climbing that mountain have the patience to do it with consistency and skill.

What is faith and patience? When I say have faith and patience, I am not talking about sitting around. Faith is action that knows it has nothing to fear or worry about. Patience is like the water as it hits the sand. Patience is peaceful action that can flow and keep its balance. Patience gets the right results at the right time. Action follows faith. When you are faithful, you are in action.

Faith and patience are not passive. Having faith is making a strong choice, just as having patience is a way you decide to react to any given situation. Patience can accomplish many things because patience knows how to take the time to work for the right results.

I asked worry to get me a drink of water. Worry took too long and wasn't any good at keeping me company. I asked faith to get me a drink of water. Faith smiled at me and gave me enough water to last me for the week! I think faith is much better company than worry on any day of the week! Worry is still sitting on the couch looking at me. Faith has moved on to do greater things. Be thankful. No need to hold on to worry, worry just sits around while the rest happens.

Life is happening all around you. Life doesn't stop because you're depressed or upset. I know, sometimes you just want to rest and not worry anymore, so don't! Choose to walk and live with faith and your heart will be joyous. Faith will be a much better companion than worry. When disaster strikes, worry is afraid and can't handle it. Faith can handle anything, because faith doesn't count on its own power. Faith has tapped into the unlimited power source. Nothing is impossible for God, and when you come to that realization, there is nothing to worry about!

I will not fill my soul with anxiety, hatred, pride, selfishness, or any of the things that don't leave room for love. I will be active and I will not be held back by depression, sickness, or sadness. I will enjoy this day. Tomorrow will be better because of all the positive and productive actions that I am taking today. Yesterday will leave me better and better memories. I think of whatever builds me up, instead of what tears me down. I meditate on good things.

Wake up to soberness! Get something accomplished other than running your mouth! Actions speak, while words just keep you talking when you could be walking! Now walk it out!

This is another day and each day is a new chance to change your life for the better. If you're complaining, go to the back of the line because that is exactly where you will be. But if you are moving, move on up to the front, because life is full of movement! Improvement daily is the key!

Impossible showed up at my door today and helped me move a mountain. Joy made me smile and amazing is in front of me constantly. Faith, hope and love: These three will make your spirit rich.

I am inspired today. I have this magical, whimsical feeling. It is as if joy and happiness are simmering in my soul. Wisdom has been brought to the surface and my heart is honoring the more important things. So, the trivial trials of my life have faded away, the baseless worries have disappeared, and I feel a great deal of peace. The physical world tricks us into being so stuck on seeing that we miss the real picture.

Show me 10 good reasons why I shouldn't do something. Tell me 10 reasons I can't do something and give me every reason not to even try to do it. I promise you I will not only do it, but I will do it again, and again, and again.

People at times will doubt you or the possibility of you accomplishing something. This may be because they didn't go after their dreams, or they let fear hold them back. Tune the voices of doubt out of your life. Believe in yourself. When you're on your way to success people will tell you that you can't make it. When you do make it they will say you won't last, so expect it! In the midst of that chatter stay the course and perform at your best. Mold every move with complete and absolute confidence, regardless of what is in front of you. You must see the reality of your dreams and keep moving. Greatness is faith and action in the midst of opposition!

I love the night sky, the way darkness wraps around the moon and just when you think you haven't seen enough light, a star shines at you. Although at times we walk through the darkness of life, there is always light and beauty in it. So, I say, look towards the light for soon it will be day.

No matter where you are or how dark it seems, there is light. Find a way to maneuver your way to the light. You may need to find a way to climb out of a deep well of despair. The only way you can do that is by keeping your attention on the light at the top. By continuing your focus on the light, you will find a way to reach it and bask in it.

Live in the power of today. Everything passes. Life passes us by so enjoy this moment. Get really wrapped up into now. What can I do now, today, that can make my life better tomorrow? Happiness is very active and alive. Each day you must be very active and alive in whatever way you can be and you will succeed.

Living in the moment is majestic. When you are living in the moment, you are operating in the divine power of creation. Your life is being discovered in each moment you walk through it. People that are happy know how to focus on today and tap into the magic of being a conscious part of evolving and living. When you are constantly looking back at something, you miss out on the joy of the transformation you are going through at every moment. Adjust your channel and tune into the movie your life is playing today. No more reruns. We all want a do over or a clean slate. You have one today so make the best of it. Tune into how you feel and what you are thinking right now. Be awake and aware of your surroundings so that you can actively take part in the shaping of your very own existence.

Every day say thank you at least 100 times! Be thankful and smile often. Count your blessings, not your mistakes. Count your blessings, not your regrets. Count your blessings, not the things you want. Count your blessings; always be in a state of thankfulness.

It is imperative to love the things you have and to appreciate where you are. If you're not thankful for all that you have now, how can you be thankful for more? You mirror your attitude in your life. If you are on welfare, be thankful for that provision. Life is full of transitions. Know that you are just passing through; change is the muse of life. Nothing stays the same and we can grow through anything and be in a completely different place in the blink of an eye. If you have a mate, and your relationship isn't what you want it to be, don't put that energy into your home. Be loving toward your mate and think about the good things they do and just how thankful you are to have them. Be thankful that you have two hands and two feet. Be happy you are breathing. When you become thankful for your blessings, they will multiply and you will discover the abundant treasures in and around you.

We were made for the extraordinary. We are not average, we are exceptional. We crave miracles!

I went to a religious service and this is the message I received. It had an enlightening movement throughout my spirit. I realized that everything on my mind at that moment was meant for me. I knew that I should strive for what I wanted, not what I thought I could get. I came to grasp that I had been short changing myself by not reaching for the extraordinary. On that day, my understanding flew to a higher level. I made a list of all the things I wanted. I challenged myself to extend toward what I really wanted, and I got it. I was persuaded and encouraged to live life in the sky, instead of on the ground. I married that thought to the fact that I knew there are no limits for divine things. So now I know to always strive for the extraordinary because that is what I am meant for and that is what I am. That is what all of us are. As soon as we start recognizing that, we will walk down the path of extraordinary daily.

Your success isn't measured by sight. Your success is in the spirit you show and in the happiness you feel.

Success is not about how big your house is or what kind of car you have. It isn't about how beautiful or handsome your mate is. It isn't about where you went to school or where your children went to school. While all of these things can reflect success that you have in your life, within themselves they are not success. Success is not measured by how many things you have or bragging rights. If I gave you a million dollars, could you claim success from that? No. It is very important not to get into the *who has more* game. This will ultimately lead to a life filled with achievements and accomplishments but without the feeling that comes with success. I like the part in *Cat on a Hot Tin Roof* when Paul Newman tells his father that he didn't get love from him, he got things. He also said that those things didn't mean anything to him. That is true for everyone. Just having things does not make you successful.

Success is really measured by how happy your life is. Having a home full of love shows a great level of success in your life. If you are happy being a cook, then cook. You can still be successful if you don't exactly do the work you like to do, but those that get to do the work they like to do tend to be happier. Happiness is a great way to measure success. You can be a great provider, but you may change your job to do what you love to do. When people do what they enjoy daily that leads to success. Let your own happiness tell you that you are a great success!

You keep going. You keep smiling. You keep fighting the fight. You keep on loving. Repetition can keep you sane.

I'm not talking about being stuck in a rut, and I'm not talking about boredom. Routine can lead you through moments when you feel that life is abstruse. I know that I take a shower in the morning, fix my hair and groom myself daily. Clinging to that kind of simplicity at times can give me the mental supervision I need to bridge me to the next moment. I know that food is a necessity to life, and so I plan that in my day. I know that I maintain a clean home. These are good things to rely on daily. There are times when you will feel confused or lost and you may not know how to climb out of that feeling. That is exactly when you rely on the basics of life. So I say start with making your bed every morning when you wake up.

I will not judge today, I will observe and learn from people. I will not get offended. Instead, I will realize that people are just being who they are and I will let them be the way they are. I will keep my peace and let no one disturb it. I will walk in joy of heart and peace of spirit! I will try to show generosity in all I do.

Many times we internalize too much! Just watch people. Really look at them and observe. You will find out very quickly that they are in their own world and that the way they treat you is based on that. Let people be. Instead of judging, attempt to understand everything around you.

We all have that one thing that we tell ourselves will make everything okay if we get it. You don't need that guy, that house, or that money. When you get it all and the newness of it wears off, you will still be you.

Smile today and act as though you have whatever you are waiting for to be happy—now. When you do that, you can tap into that joy and show you have faith that you will receive it. You will also see that you are still the same person and that happiness comes from within. I could give you everything on your wish list and you will still deal with the thoughts you have right now. You will still have the same name. Take everything away from me and I am still the same person. Give me the world and I am the same person with the world. When you realize this, you will grow and be happy right where you are. This is the time in your life to rejoice daily and to smile. Now is the time!

You have three incredible, miraculous and amazing things that have already happened to you today. First, you woke up this morning. Second, you're breathing. Third, you can walk, talk, or swim (or you can do all three of these things). So you may have six gifts! What will you do with your gifts?

Did you get the point? Some of you may be thinking, 'But I can't swim.' Then, some of you are thinking, 'I have so much that I have been given today.' You wake up with blessings. God gave us the tools to go out and get what we want out of life. It is the use of those tools that will help us get the most out of every day and out of life.

Do what you love, that is what you live for. Money will come but when you put money first, you lose the joy. You can't take it with you. The only thing you can really keep are your experiences, so love them!

When you're just doing whatever you can to make money, you feel empty and only as good as your next dollar. We spend money, we can't keep it. The one thing that does belong to us is what we experience. When you think of your day and smile, that is a good thing. Your memories are your true possessions.

This is the best and only moment of my life. I can't change yesterday or live in tomorrow. I can only breathe the air I am breathing today. I am here, right now. I could give you the kiss of my life right now, because this is my life. I could love you here and now because this is where I am and I'm alive now. I feel everything I will ever feel right now.

Stop for a moment and look at your skin, your hair, the shape of your lips. Look at the way your jeans fit. Look at the way your eyes light up when you smile. You have everything you need right now to give love and receive it. Go out and tell the people in your life that you love them. If you kissed the one you have romantic affection for right now, and you concentrate on breathing and the way you're looking and feeling right now, it will be the kiss of your life because this moment is your life.

I want you to put on your armor today and go win your battle. Put on your shine today and be somebody's light. Enjoy this day. Forget about yesterday, but learn from it! Plan for tomorrow but think about today!

Sometimes you won't know how in the world you will be able to do something. You might look out like a soldier of an army of 300 going against an army of 10,000 and think that there is no way. But faith knows there is a way. The battle may not even be what you thought. So step out like an insanely brave soldier and fight anyway, you will make it.

Make decisions you can be proud of. In the end, you won't care what car you drove, what clothing you wore. It won't be about how many people knew you. It's going to be about the lives you've touched, the people you've

helped. You will be proud of all the times you made the right choices, even when you didn't want to. I want to be proud of me. In the end, that's what I want.

We are all faced with daily decisions that really, in the end, are going to be what make or break us. So make decisions you can look back on with pride. You can make the decision to clean your house daily, and you will look back on that decision and be proud of it. You can decide to go to school and be a good student, and you will look back and be proud of that decision. Make decisions that will make you proud of yourself.

I care and I know there are so many others who care, too. If you're looking for that light, that love, or that hand, it is there. If we care when we are so small in God's eyes, certainly, God cares.

As you reach out and become more involved at work, at home, at school and in your community, you will see that there are many who care and who care about you. There are people out there right now that want to help you. If you are looking for someone who cares, we are there, just reach out.

What would the world be like if there was no laughter? Today, be thankful for laughter by finding the humor in things. Smile a lot, laugh a lot. It does the heart good! Always be ready to have your own great time and create your own sunshine! Know how to feel joyous and let that feeling last. Once you tap into it, you will be able to tap into it again and again.

Smile and laugh as much as you can! Let things tickle you more. When your co-worker does the same thing that gets on your nerves, find the humor in it. Find the humor in the picture of life and it will brighten things up for you every day!

Get out of your head right now! Go past everything you have seen. Get past your knowledge and your wisdom. Connect to the greater wisdom in the heavens and in the universe. Stop thinking you can't handle this, you can't do that, or that you are limited by money or ability. THIS ISN'T ABOUT YOU! When you realize that, everything will turn into 'I can and it will happen!'

This isn't about you! You have to get out of your head. You're in your house, in your issues, in your sickness, in your bed, in your tears, in your filth. You have got to move out of that place. Move to the wisdom and love from above. When you are operating in that, all things are possible. I don't know what religion you are so call it what you will, but I will call it God. God is the source of all things. You disconnect when you get into yourself. Get out of yourself and watch the world around you. It isn't about your car, your dinner, or your house. It is about greatness and all things working out for the good of all. It's about tapping into the power in the universe. Our universe has been made full of endless power and energy. Get into the love that you can find all over the world.

Today, I challenge you to make a list of 10 of your strengths or best qualities. Meditate on them and walk in those things. Then write down something you're going to accomplish today and make sure to strive to complete it. As you go through your day, think of how you can give and how you can grow. Make sure to pat yourself on the back and be proud of each step you make in the right direction.

Always be prepared and plan for success. Set your mind and heart on the right things to meditate on when you start your day.

Just live. Say how you feel in the nicest or most creatively positive way you can. But sometimes, just blurt it out. When someone or something moves you, don't be afraid to feel it or to act on it. Fall in love everyday with everything, including your loved ones. I SAY LIVE AT THE TOP OF YOUR LUNGS, then sometimes at a soft whisper but always deliberately! Can you handle that?!

Your life is shaped by the choices that you make, so make strong choices. You are reaping the consequences of what you say and what you do; that gives you more of a reason to really say how you feel or do what you truly want to do. If I am being me, I know I am attracting a more satisfying life. I know that if I am authentic in the way I live, that my life will be more pleasant because it will reflect what's truly in my heart.

TRIALS MAKE US STRONGER

"YOU DON'T HAVE TO MAKE THE SUN—IT'S ALREADY BEEN MADE. YOU DON'T HAVE TO SUSTAIN LIFE ON THE EARTH. YOU JUST HAVE TO BE THE BEST YOU THAT YOU CAN BE. IT'S WORTH FIGHTING FOR SOMETHING YOU BELIEVE IN. IT'S WORTH STRUGGLING FOR SOMETHING TO BE BETTER. YOU WERE MADE WITH THE NEED TO CREATE AND TO BE SOMEONE YOU CAN BE PROUD OF. YOUR OBSTACLES ARE YOUR OPPORTUNITIES TO GROW."

I sat down with pain today and asked the million dollar question. I asked, "Why?" Pain took my hand and said, "You can help others, because you know me." Pain said there are others suffering, in need of empathy and love. Pain said that I could experience the joy of walking beside them, and that joy would wipe away my pain. Pain told me the answer is love, that the answer to all life's questions is love.

When you apply pressure to gold, the pressure gets rid of the impurities and refines the gold. If you stomp on a bag of honey, you will find sweetness. When loving eyes cry, it causes the soul to be polished and brightened. Ah, yes, my pain bows to my kindness and love. My pain stands in awe at my courage.

There is beauty in imperfection. There is something exhilarating about not knowing what's going to happen all the time. There is a cleansing about tears that feels good. There is something great about feeling fear when you face it. Divinity can be found even in the worst of moments. It's that it made you grow; it made people around you advance. It molded you into who you are. It

transformed fear into a feeling you can manage and maneuver through. Now you know you can do it.

When you are amidst grief, you must find a place of shelter in knowing that growth will come out of it. That somehow that pain will transcend into a majestic beauty that touches your soul. Looking back, sometimes we regret the things in life that shaped us. What you have been through formed you into who you are and it helps you relate to others better. Turn your tragedy into joy by helping others with the knowledge and strength you have.

When under stress, it is not time to be discouraged! As the proverb says, if you are discouraged in the day of distress, you will lack power. This is the time you will need the most power. So fill yourself with love, faith and hope. Keep in mind that nothing is impossible for love to fix or change! Stand strong, you are not tired, you are not depressed, you are not angry. You are covering everything with love and that gives you power!

When your spirit is powerful, you will be able to work through things and see the way out of trouble. When your spirit is low, you break. We all can think back at times we have been under pressure and we didn't let it bring us down or frighten us. We can also think of times we have allowed anger, depression, or impatience to weaken our strength. When we stay encouraged, we have the strength to face any situation before us.

I know what it's like to feel pain. I know what it's like to want to just sleep. I'm thankful for the darkness God let me suffer because it put me in such beautiful light. You

will make it through this. You are much stronger than you think.

My intensity, my honesty, my love, my courage, my wisdom all come from walking in moments I can hardly write about. I am so glad I came from a story, a struggle. I smile now because I have come so far. I have been prepared for this. I am thankful for being found worthy to go through it. I had the strength for it. I was made for the battle. In times when prayer is needed, strength and answers are given.

Do not let the problem you see bring you down. As I said before, discouragement will rob you of all your power. Know that things always work out. Remember the things you worried about last year, they worked out. It will all work out, this day, this month, this year. Have faith! I am so sure it will work out that I can say it has already passed. Feel that way inside.

How you feel is so important. It isn't what's going on in your life; it's how you feel about it. I could talk to two people in the same situation, one would tell me everything is going to work out and the good things about their situation. One would be looking at the wind telling me how bad it is. When we are looking at the wind, it will slow us down. There is nothing like going up a mountain with a big backpack on your back. Discouragement slows us down, sometimes so much that we can't do anything. Do not let yourself be discouraged. Stop looking at the wind. Look ahead, look at the light at the end of the tunnel, it is always there.

Being grounded doesn't mean you always know what to do. Being strong doesn't mean you always have the strength. Being wise doesn't mean you always make the

right choice. But having faith is always turning to God. And God will never forsake you. Just let go of it. And it's okay to cry. After the rain, there is a rainbow. After tears, there is a smile.

You can be doing all the right things and you will still have times when you feel like your back is against the wall. You will still have times when tears fall. But, after the rain, the rainbow appears in your life. Let the storm pass and watch the sun shine things up. There is great power from just smiling. So, when you have that moment and you're on the floor crying and praying, after you let that out, smile. There is always hope and hope knows that the good is coming, that the answer is already on its way. It's okay to cry sometimes. We all do it.

Tears don't mean what we think they do. They don't mean we have lost or that we are hurt beyond repair. They don't mean we can't handle things or that we are weak. Tears are a washing away of things we don't need in our lives. The problem is when we invite the same tears back into our lives.

Don't keep inviting pain to revisit you. If you party with pain, most likely at the end of the night, you won't be happy. When pain knocks on your door you don't have to answer.

Life isn't about avoidance. Life is about facing it, learning from it, figuring out that you're powerful enough to conquer it. Life is about asking for help, being faithful, believing and working to make the changes you need in your life.

Some people will do anything to avoid getting hurt or being hurt over something. Having the goal in life to avoid pain at all costs, will not help you succeed. The real goal in life is to learn from everything. We all need to grow and the truth is that pain and the hard times in life can make us grow the most. So don't create pain or think pain, but know that your life is about learning from everything. As you proceed in the process of becoming the best version of yourself, if you get hurt along the way, that's okay. You will recover! Happiness comes hand-in-hand with growth.

Say the things that are hard for you to say. Do the things that are hard for you to do. Have courage and face the tough issues. Don't be afraid of a little discomfort. Stop wasting time and delaying your happiness. God will not let you handle beyond what you can bare. This too shall pass. Live your life with honesty. Be who you are. No regrets.

Easy isn't always better. Do the hard things; life will get easier. Don't look for the fast way, look for the right way. Don't look for easy because easy can fall apart quickly.

When you are in the wrong relationship, you know it. When you are doing the wrong things, you know it. When you aren't being honest, you know it. I say the hard things to say. I had to tell my family and friends that I didn't feel the way they did about life. I left the religion of my youth and it took me about 10 years to recover from that. But I did recover. I lost having my mother and my sisters in my life. I also lost my whole community but I gained the 'me' that was so lost. I went into a deep depression. But I can tell you now that I would do it all again, because I have to live in honesty. I cannot go through the motions and tell you what you want to hear because that is a slow and painful death. It doesn't matter if you like my life, I have to live it. The only way you can enjoy your life is if you live in honesty.

These are the days I will always look back on and see the beauty in. I will remember the struggle and smile. I will remember running like crazy and smile. I will remember the anticipation of the unknown. I will be thankful that I had the courage to stand for my belief and faith in God. I will look back and be proud of caring for others and wanting to help in any way I can. I fight for my son, my future and the future of many. I fight for every person to stand and to succeed in life.

I have a depth and strength to me because of being a single mother at this time. I say that because I know that will change soon enough. I will appreciate the blessings from the growth of this experience. I have strength from those moments I cried and wished I had a partner. I remember being pregnant and wishing I had someone to help me carry my groceries. I remember wanting someone to be there with me. God gave me the help I needed and beautified me in my weakness. I gained more empathy and sympathy for others. I was able to talk to other women and give them sound advice. I helped strengthen others by still smiling and feeling good about myself. I helped others by letting them see me have strength in my weakness.

Love believes all things. It's dangerous when you stop believing, it can separate you from recognizing love. You want to be full grown in spirit, yet remain a child at heart. When you fall victim to pain, it's difficult not to hide in it, but don't stop believing in the magic of life because it is still here.

Regardless of what you have been through, don't stop believing that miracles do happen! Don't stay in the pain you've been through or are going through at present. When you freeze pain in time, it can be agonizing. When you keep reliving it over and over again, it can completely crush you. Get past it, grow from it and move on. Know that miracles are coming to you and happening to you daily. Start looking for the things that just seem to work out somehow. Don't miss out on the magic in your life by being imprisoned by pain. Divorce yourself from pain and move forward to all the good that is here for you.

You get to a point when your heart is unbreakable. When you've already felt such intense agony and abandonment, that nothing can ever hurt you again. Not that you won't get hurt, but that you won't let it hurt you.

After you have been through enough, you no longer worry about being broken. No one can threaten you with heartbreak; you've been there. You know now that nothing can break you. I know that no matter what tomorrow brings I can handle it. I have walked in places I didn't think I would and I am thankful for that. I have walked through troublesome places. I know that, regardless of what is thrown my way, God will bring me through it.

Faith sees that which cannot be seen. Faith sees that the impossible, that the dream you have, is not only possible but has already happened. Faith is that sure. Walk by faith, not by sight. Being faithful means you believe in the process. Many of us miss out on blessings because we are holding on to what we want and fighting the process. Faith says that we give into the process and know that our work is not in vain.

Faith is the medicine for every trial. You know how kids like you to kiss their boo boos. Well, faith kisses all your wounds. Faith knows the good has already arrived. You are already saved, safe and well. It's over; faith says the trial has passed.

Once you realize that you are not in control, you will feel more controlled and more at peace. You will stop fighting what you are afraid of. Your hand will open up and you will loosen your grip. You will let go of past pain and you will step into your wonderful life.

It doesn't matter what goes on in your life, what disappointments you may have had, or what changes you go through. When you have love in your heart and in your spirit, you will always feel joy. In the midst of tears, fears, trials, or pain, you can still feel joy. Love is healing and joy is love's bandage. Love puts joy on a wound and it heals.

Sometimes it's good to just be silent. Don't complain all the time. Don't tell your partner to listen constantly. You've already said it, just try waking up and being happy each day. In silence, let things settle. The sun rose without you telling it to. Wipe your head of worries. Let your mind be silent and your heart be full of love.

When you're silent, you're listening. Sometimes you need to listen. Listen to your surroundings, listen to the voice of love inside you. You can say the same things to people over and over again and they can turn a deaf ear to it. Talk in a different way, talk through silence.

Everything takes balance. If you're not in balance, you cannot walk. When you're balanced and centered, you will stop crawling and you will walk with certainty.

Our trials can help us see where we need to be more balanced and they can help us gain the strength we need to walk with certainty.

Sometimes things happen and you have no control over them. So, you kick and scream but there is no use in telling a tree to move, it has been planted there. You don't always need to fight everything. Fight the mountain, but let the tree be. Pick your battles.

Many times we let the smallest things bother us. You may call your friend because your sister said she was better at something than you are. You might even talk about that for the entire day. Just let that go, it is only distracting you from the bigger and better things in your life. It may be distracting you from putting your energy into moving the mountain in front of you. You may not be able to advance in your job because you're so busy being worried about the little things. Let the little things go and work to change the things in your life that are in need of change.

The man or woman in the mirror is the only one you can change. So, it was really your brother's fault, right? If only your mom and dad did a better job of being parents. It's all the prejudice in the world right? You can only change you, Stop shifting blame and take responsibility for you. You can complain or change your life.

I did something that I didn't think I was able to do. There is something I really wanted with my heart and God said no. In the past, I wouldn't have let go. I have given into God without kicking and screaming. No, I kicked and screamed a little. Many times we hurt ourselves because

we hold on to what we know God has said to let go of. No need to be in pain, wipe your tears away and let go.

It isn't what we do when we get what we want or when things seem to go our way. It's smiling and having faith when things look like they are going any way but the way you want them to. It's when what you want is taken away from you, when God says no. What are you going to do? Not break down, not kick and scream. You let go and let God, having faith. Stop looking through the eyes of your heart and look through the eyes of faith. Let go of what you're trying to hold on to. Stop hanging off the mountain, just let go and you'll land on your feet. And when you do, the mountain of a problem will be gone and what is yours will be standing there ready for you! When you let go, you will be surprised to see that what you wanted so badly may have already been yours. It just might have needed time to come to you.

You know how everything looks so much smaller when you're looking out the window of an airplane? Well, guess what? Your obstacles or problems are a lot smaller than they look from your vantage point. Just as the sun is a lot bigger than it may seem when you look up into the sky. The brightness and blessings in your life are so much more than you know!

We can't always see the big picture. We may think things should have worked out a certain way and get so stuck on that, that we miss out on the real gift. Your blessing is even bigger and better than what you thought. When you finally see the big picture, you will know why it happened that way.

I shall woe you on this mountain top and rescue you from this sea of endless drifting, of endless wants and

needs. I say dream and live in that dream regardless of what you see before you. Know that your needs are met and what you want is yours, so you have nothing to want for. All things are available to you, so call them to you by faith.

The times in life that have tested me the most, have directed my heart and soul to greater depths of knowledge, wisdom and beauty. You can do this, whatever it is. You are strong and you can endure so much more than you give yourself credit for. You are made in brilliance, and in God's power all things can be conquered. I pray that you see just how truly impressive you are.

I saw a mountain and after God moved it there was no hole in the ground. It completely disappeared and a rose grew there. The grass around it grew tall and healthy. The soil underneath it was moist and fresh like the day. There was a constant light that shone on the rose. Whatever mountain you are facing is hiding a rose underneath it. When you find that rose, it will add growth and beauty to you that is life changing.

When God removes something he just doesn't remove it, he puts something better there. The spiritual growth in my life is undeniable. Face everything you are going through with the anticipation of seeing what is hidden behind or underneath the problem or issue. There is a rose that awaits you. There is nothing like true happiness and that comes from a spiritual state of mind and a joyous heart. God has to explain things to you by showing you and helping you understand wisdom in your spirit.

OVERCOMING DEPRESSION

"DEPRESSION IS A STATE OF MIND. WE CAN PRACTICE DEPRESSION OR WE CAN PRACTICE HAPPINESS. WE CAN PRACTICE HAPPINESS BY WHAT WE MEDITATE ON IN OUR MIND AND HEART."

Depression comes from thoughts; you can change your thoughts!

Depression is all about what you do and what you think. If you are unhappy, think to yourself, what is the voice in my head telling me?

Everyone can enjoy happiness, you can get where you want to go by practicing happiness. Happiness is an inner state of contentment. We can't be happy if we are not where we want to be, or if we are not on a path to get there. We cannot be happy if we do not like who we are.

Some of the most talented, wealthiest, most famous individuals in the world were in the circumstances you face today, but they knew they could get anywhere they wanted to go if they believed in themselves and worked toward it. My father couldn't read when he got married to my mother at 18 years of age. Now, my father is a walking Webster's dictionary with a vocabulary that would challenge the most educated people in the world. Anything you believe, you can achieve. Faith can move mountains of obstacles and place you in the space you want to occupy.

Many don't believe it but I had horrible self-esteem growing up and it carried into my early adulthood. I always had this feeling that I didn't measure up. I thought I was unlovable, can you believe that? I didn't even think I was worth loving. I didn't know my own value. I suffered from severe depression because I didn't like myself, I didn't like where I was, and I didn't know how to get where I wanted to go.

So, I found myself feeling lost and I didn't know what to do. I started to read books, and I found out something so amazing. I found out that I could practice happiness. I could think different thoughts, I could believe in myself, love myself, and that I could get where I wanted to be. I started turning down the voices in my head that said, "You're not good enough, you're not loved, you can't do anything right," and I replaced them with, "You're good enough, you can do anything, you are loved." Thinking differently changed my life. I started to realize that much of my life was a result of the meditations of my mind and heart. I started to replace every negative or unhappy statement with a positive statement about myself and my life. I was on my way to learning how to practice happiness by thinking good thoughts.

Next, I started to take the necessary steps to make headway in getting to where I wanted to go. I started doing simple things like making my bed daily because I knew that it was important to live in a clean environment. I started to study and really take advantage of any educational opportunities before me. It didn't matter what it was. If I could think of it, I told myself I could do it. When you start believing in yourself and telling yourself that you can do it, you will meet every challenge successfully.

When we stop fearing failure, we can't help but succeed. Set reachable goals and as you reach them, check them off your mental list. Celebrate every little step you successfully take, build up your own self-worth. You will see that your circumstances start to change and this will excite you.

In this process, it is very important to keep a positive attitude. I see people get in their own way by thinking that everything will turn out badly and that everything *is* so bad. This thought process will turn into depression.

When you think that everything is so bad and that is how everything will turn out, that is how it will be. It's like asking bad things to follow you. Stay emotionally strong. Don't let anyone or anything knock you off balance! You can see your life as one problem after another or as one solution after another. You can be the calm after the storm or you can be the storm. You can be faithful or you can be fearful. Have peace in knowing all is working out! Why does the ending of your story have to be sad? Write a happy story everyday in your mind and watch all the positive things that happen!

Write yourself notes and put them on your mirror; write them on your cell phone. You can write positive thoughts on flash cards and hide them all around your house to discover them later. They can say things like, "All good things are coming to me. Life is good. I enjoy every moment. I am lovable, and I am worth more than gold." You can also say you are doing or have the things that you want. An example of this is: "I am a very successful teacher. I eat healthy and exercise. My body looks good. I love my new home. It has everything I need and wanted." As they say, whatever a man thinks of himself, he becomes that. So think good thoughts!

Live in a healthy environment. Take in light and the darkness will start to disappear!

Our environment is very important to examine in order to overcome depression. If you are in a situation where you are being abused, or if you have been abused, you need to seek help and deal with it. Look at your home and make sure you are living in a clean environment. Tell those that are around you to speak to you in a loving and respectful manner and do the same in return. Read spiritual and uplifting literature. Watch and listen to things that inspire and encourage you. If you take in mental junk food, your mind will be polluted with unhealthy thoughts. If you take in spiritual and uplifting thoughts, your mind will get cleaned up.

Don't think of depression as you. You are not depressed. You are thinking and feeling a certain way and you can change that. You can be a happy, healthy individual because you choose to be.

FORGIVENESS

"WHEN I FORGIVE OTHERS, I HELP MYSELF. WHEN I AM HARD ON OTHERS, IT MAKES IT HARD ON ME. WHEN I HOLD ON TO BAD FEELINGS, IT HURTS ME. WHEN I LET GO AND FORGIVE, I FEEL BETTER AND LIVE A HEALTHIER LIFE!"

It isn't about you; it's about them!

When people do unkind things, it is because they are unhappy. I have listened to people complain over and over about how much certain people don't like them or treat them poorly. Many of us think we are the reason for bad treatment, but that is not the case. Someone who is happy is loving and kind. Someone who is not happy will be unkind and angry. When someone is unkind or angry, you should feel sorry for them. People act the way they feel. So, if someone acts badly, they feel bad. If someone acts good, they feel good.

Be calm and let things go when you can.

When someone is lashing out at you, the best thing to do in many cases is to remain calm. If it's just words, you may say something back that is kind and overlook what they have said because you know what they are going through, or that they are not as mature spiritually as you are. There is a time to just overlook things and keep showing love. There is also a time to stay clear of those who continually hurt you. Be wise in showing love to others. Forgive.

God forgives and forgets. We remember and remember and make people prove things to us. That isn't forgiveness. We are not the judge. Give people you know a clean slate every single day.

Again, you should always show balance. True forgiveness doesn't keep bringing the same thing up over and over again. True forgiveness also doesn't treat someone bad and make them feel like they owe you. That isn't forgiveness at all. When you forgive someone, you don't call the same thing to mind every time you see them.

Let people change. Give the people in your life a chance to be different and better. Don't bring up what they did 20 years ago. Let's say someone went to jail for stealing. They can stop stealing. They can turn around and change, so let them. We all need mercy. We have all done things that we wish we had not done. We have all been shown mercy and so we should show mercy to each other. There is no need to label someone because of something they have done. Why remind everybody else about what someone did wrong? When we do this, we are making a judgment and none of us have the right to judge. If God remembered everything bad we have done, we wouldn't have a chance. God concentrates on the good we do and with a breath of kindness, blows away our past. Let's give each other a chance for a future by forgiving.

Stop beating yourself up! We all fall down, just get up.

Sometimes we are great at forgiving others but have such a hard time forgiving ourselves. We may blame ourselves and punish ourselves, when God actually forgave us. It's better to turn around, or get up than to tell yourself you're such a bad person. Forgiving yourself is just as important as forgiving others.

Just when you start to think you are such a great person and you wouldn't ever do something someone else did, watch out because you are human, too. Be careful about

the advice you give . . . you just might find out that you can't take your own advice.

Sometimes we tend to look at someone who has done something we think is so bad with disgust and treat them like they aren't even human anymore. We have no idea that they are so sorry and beating themselves up and are experiencing great pain over it. We don't need to punish others or treat them like a leper because we haven't walked a day in their shoes. Always show love. It takes a big person to act in a forgiving, loving way. You will notice that when you do this, you might see tears in someone's eyes because they are so touched by the love you have shown them.

We know so much about what we think, how we think, and about our experience. The real beauty is stepping outside of that. We shut the door of our tender compassion and we become a *me* society. If it is *we* instead of *me*, we would succeed.

We can only come from our experience, so no, we probably don't understand why people or communities do what they do. It's not all about what we think. Once you see everyone through your eyes, through your ways, you will start to shut yourself off from others. It's not about *me*, it's about *we*.

When we forgive, it actually will help us to be healthier and happier. Look for the good in people and concentrate on that!

Holding on to hurt feelings can make your spirit ill. You can do more harm holding on to the hurt and not forgiving than if you forgive. You can think about something that hurt you for months, not talking to someone, blaming someone. When you finally confront them, you may find out that they didn't even think they hurt you like that, or they weren't thinking about it. Don't hold on to hurt, it can be toxic.

If God were like you, would there be a world? Would there be time for people to learn love? How long would you give them? How much time do you give people now? We all need more patience, more love, more tender affection for each other and more empathy.

There is always room for more forgiveness. We see how many wars we have had and we can see that if it was up to humans the world may have been destroyed a long time ago. God teaches us forgiveness.

Peter asked Jesus how many times he should forgive. He thought he was being generous when asked if it should be up to seven times! Jesus told him that he should forgive up to 70 times seven! (Matthew 18:21, 22) In other words, we shouldn't count how many times people sin against us and we should forgive over and over again.

Do we mentally have a chalkboard of everyone's names and checks next to their names to represent how many times he or she has done something wrong? Do we see people and instantly remember things they have done to us? We can all probably answer 'Yes' in many cases. This is something we all need to work on. God does this so much better than we do. That is why God's love for us is so strong. Each time we come in prayer, God doesn't think about the last thing we did wrong, or what we are going to ask for this time.
Unfortunately, many times we do this to each other. Instead, we could let each experience with every individual be as new as the day.

A man owed a king $10 million. He could not pay the debt, so the king ordered that he be sold along with his family. But the man fell before the king and begged him to be patient. The king felt pity for him and forgave his debt. But the man left the king and went to a man who owed him $2,000 and threw him in jail until the debt could be paid. (Matt. 18:23-34) God forgives us. Do we forgive each other?

In comparison to what we owe God, others owe us very little, if anything. God could lock us in jail and throw away the key. God could say exactly why that is a just punishment for us. Yet, God is patient with us. Should we not be patient with each other? If you went to God and said you would never forgive your next-door neighbor because they did something that was actually very bad, would this make sense when we compare what that person owes us in comparison to what we owe God? It is wisdom to forgive and loving to forget.

SELF-ESTEEM

"DON'T WORRY ABOUT BEING TOO THIS OR TOO THAT. JUST BE YOU! BE THE UNCUT VERSION OF YOURSELF. BE AUTHENTIC AND REAL. YOU WILL BE ADMIRED BY MANY FOR HAVING THE COURAGE TO BE YOURSELF."

Be the best at being you. I promise no one can do it better! I had a run-in with someone that made me realize how much I've changed. I don't get offended so easily anymore. I appreciate the best in me and no one can try to change that because of their own insecurities. I will break into my superwoman at anytime! No word is powerful unless you believe it! Believe in yourself and your

abilities. Protect yourself by knowing how great you are on the way to where you're going!

Nobody is working on you if you're trying to be someone else. Love your differences, even the things you may not like about yourself, love them. When I started to love myself for being too spirited sometimes or too protected at times, I started to know who I was and I started to change. I also started to balance things I did naturally to make them work for me. You have got to be you, not someone else. You will start to be better when you feel better about you.

When I was the perfect me, people couldn't see me. When I just started to be exactly who I am and let people see me make mistakes, people started to love me.

A sign of good self-esteem is taking rejection well.

What's wrong with rejection? If you feel good about you, then rejection should slide right off of your back. Just remember, they don't know what they are missing. If someone turns you down for a date, if you get fired, if a group of people doesn't want to be friends with you, so what! At least you know that wasn't for you. No one can tell you your worth but you. No situation or rejection can bring down your value. Know that there is only one of you, that you are a diamond and no one can dim your shine but you.

I challenge you today to ask three people for something you want that you don't think they will give you. There are three things that could happen: 1) You may get three rejections, 2) One person may say 'Yes', or 3) You may get three things you didn't know you could get. What is there to lose?

You will miss out if you don't take chances. It's better to reach than to hold back and miss out. You will also find that you will win so much more by putting yourself out there and letting people see you. We all know there is nothing to fear except fear.

I went to a subway yesterday and this man just flat out gave me one of the best compliments I've ever gotten. He was willing to make a fool of himself. He let go of his ego and really looked at me and said what he had to say with feeling. I will never forget that. I respected him for not being afraid to step out a little.

People get so afraid to look stupid that they miss out on opportunities. You could miss out on the best thing that could ever happen to you if you don't risk yourself. If you want great things to happen to you, then you have to sacrifice greatly. If people are looking for your flaws, they will find them! But the people you want and need in your life will always see the beauty in you. My greatest weakness is my greatest strength.

I used to allow a lot that I do not tolerate now, because I am a grown woman. I am a grown woman. If you missed it, I grew up. If you forgot it, let me remind you—I am a grown woman. If you think I will tolerate those things now, let me remind you—I AM A GROWN WOMAN!

When we become adults, we do not need to have the same world we did as children. If your brother picked on you when you were a child, you don't need to allow it now. If your family didn't get along when you were a child, get along now. If you felt angry often, choose not to be angry now. You are an adult; act like one!

We can look at our lives and notice that we are just living our childhood over. Whatever world you lived in as a child, you do not have to live in it now. We all have defense mechanisms that we needed to survive in our youth, in our families, in our environments. You are an adult, and you can strip those off and start being treated the way you want to be treated. You can start living the way you want to live. You don't want to be a child in big clothes. You have the power now, so use it and make your surroundings and the way you handle things better.

Stop giving yourself away. Stop looking for someone to tell you that you're beautiful. Stop looking for someone to tell you that you're worth loving. Start feeling beautiful. Start feeling and knowing that you're amazing, that you are a gift. Whoever wins your love has found a priceless treasure. Start feeling loved.

Everything starts with you. When I didn't feel loved, I couldn't receive love, or even let myself be loved. You have to start feeling the love around you, feel the admiration of who you are and others will, too. When you feel loved and know you are lovable, you will be able to see the love around you. A compliment will not mean anything to you if you don't believe it's true.

Life changes when you stop having something to prove. When you start to walk in your power of thought and feeling, you become a new you. When you no longer need validation or return for what you give, you become less needy. No one has to see me, because I see me. I don't need recognition; I don't need a trumpet blown before me. You don't have to lay out a red carpet for me to walk on. I know my value and I see my beauty.

I'm intensely honest and I fearlessly walk into every room as myself. I know who I am and I naturally have recognition because I give it to myself. I am filled with love and it pours out of me. I could walk in any room with the plainest of clothes, without the expensive jewelry and no one could outshine me. When you start to see how beautiful you are, you will not need to prove yourself to anyone. I am confident in who I am and do not need outside approval. That's growth on fire.

The more I've come to love myself, the more I've come to love others. The happier I am with myself, the happier I am with you. The less I find wrong with myself, the less I find wrong with others. I find good in me. I am a pearl. When I shine, you shine, too.

When you start to glow from an inner love for yourself, you will make others brighter, too. People will feel better around you and even act better around you. You will notice that your world brightens every time you feel joy and you smile.

Know your value! I am a diamond. I am a rare jewel. I will not just give myself away, or be in a rush to be taken off the shelf. I am in a special place and only a special person can take my heart. One thing you should always know as a lady is that you're worth loving. You're priceless! You're worth someone opening doors and pulling out chairs. You're worth a man always wanting to be there. You're worth a man holding on and not ever thinking of letting go. You're a woman to love and you are worth loving!

If you had the most beautiful diamond in the world, chances are you wouldn't put a sticker on it, tell people it's on sale to anyone and give it away to the first buyer. You are much more precious than the world's finest jewel So why put yourself on sale or even give yourself away? You shouldn't treat yourself like a piece of furniture in a store that is going out of business because chances are, if you do, people will treat you like you are nothing special. You show people how special you are by loving yourself and giving yourself dignity. Don't let someone buy you. In fact, don't let anyone buy you. You'll always be priceless in the window of life, so don't sell yourself short.

Love is strong, not weak. Love doesn't allow itself to be walked on. Love is patient and kind. Love will put up with much, but love will also stand in strength. Love is respected and honored. Loving someone doesn't mean that you become no one. Love has a reason to exist all by itself. Love isn't defined by someone. Love is sweet and good served alone.

Love is not weak and beaten up. Love is strong and resilient. Loving someone doesn't mean you love yourself less. You have to know how to love and respect yourself if you want to be capable of loving someone. If someone is going to love you, you have to demand that they respect you. If you let someone continually walk all over you, it will be hard for them to love you, because if you love yourself, you will respect yourself. Love is strong and it chooses to bend, not to break down. The loving thing may be to tell someone 'No' or that they can't treat you that way. Love does that for the love of the other person and for itself. Love is not low self-esteem.

Who knew the person I was looking for to save me was in my mirror? Who knew superwoman was me? Stop looking around for something or someone else to make

you whole. God has more faith in you than you have in yourself. You are worth more than many pearls. There is a magic that is you. Believe in you, too. I know a lot of people who believe in God, but I don't know so many who believe in themselves.

Believe in yourself, too. You could love God and love your family with all your heart, but if you don't love yourself, you will not be happy. Something will always be missing because you're missing out on you. Stop neglecting yourself and refusing to see your own beauty. It is wonderful that you take such great care of everyone and that you're the one everyone can go to for help, but that isn't enough. It is wonderful that you can see how magnificent God is but you need to also give God praise for the creation of you.

Many of us come from homes where we may not have gotten the love we needed. We may hear the voices that are around us telling us that we should be more like this or like that. But happiness is a state of mind. Happiness is feeling content with where you are every step of the way. Life is a constant journey to where we want to be. Once we reach one goal, we yearn to reach another. Fall in love with you, the real you. Instead of expecting perfection out of yourself, expect that you will be perfectly you. Once you come to understand where you are and stop judging yourself by your circumstances, you can change your circumstances. You need to know that you can go anywhere and do anything because you are capable and worth loving. God doesn't have favorites; God appreciates all of us.

No one has to appreciate it. Don't worry about who cares or if they are really getting it. You just do what you were meant to do! You share your love. You're doing it

because this is what you were called to do. When you live your life out of heart and out of depth, it's a different motivation. It's how you were made, and now you are living with purpose.

Do what you are meant to do. No one has to give you approval to be what you want to be. You're great for the way you are, the way you look, the way you walk, the way you sound, the way you talk. If I want a plant to grow, to blossom, I have to water it and take good care of it. You have to show yourself love and compassion. When you look in the mirror, you need to tell yourself that your freckles are beautiful, that your curly or straight hair is beautiful. Embrace all of the things that make you uniquely you.

Bullies are only as good as the time you give them and they are cowards by my definition. Don't give them time or reaction, don't be afraid and look at them like you are 10 feet tall. I'm much too tall to tolerate a bully.

If someone at work, school, or home is bullying you, get help! If you are being bullied, that will create low self-worth because someone is trying to beat you down. Don't tolerate bullies. Do what you have to do to make them stop!

There is a very beautiful, talented, and gifted person that will stand before you today. THAT IS YOU! YOU are that gifted and talented person! You have more than everything you need to succeed in all your endeavors today! Go get your dreams; they are waiting for you to arrive!

I don't want you to crumble, fall, or break under pressure. You're much too capable, so I want you to stop underestimating yourself. Have faith in God and have faith in the power you have been given. Rise up with wings like an eagle and fly. Don't crawl and don't walk, fly. Everything you've needed has already been yours. It's all in you, the gift is you.

We are never rejected; instead, we are protected. If someone found a treasure on the side of the road they wouldn't think it was thrown away. They would know it was lost. Trust me, the treasure that you are will be found!

Everything happens for a reason. Did you ever think that maybe it didn't work because it wasn't supposed to? You're meant to be happy and not miserable. It may have fizzled because you have inherited even better than you think. You don't even know how valuable you are. You're loved and always have been. Everyone who comes across you notices you. You just need to see it!

KNOW HOW TO BE ALONE

"I DON'T MIND BEING ALONE BECAUSE I LIKE MYSELF."

There are times in life when you must face things alone. God allows these times but God is still always by our side. God knows your full potential, and you can do so much more than you even know.

We all have that moment in life when we feel all alone and we may just be all alone for a moment. This is when we really come to have power in knowing that we are capable of so much more that we thought ourselves to be. Now, we know we are never truly alone and we can always reach out. But trials we go through that may alienate us from others can make us stronger. If we can make it through feeling alone or being alone at times, we can make it through anything!

There is something wonderful about doing things yourself, not being rescued, or having someone to protect you, being the black sheep of the family. When things go down and people need help, they come to you, because although you are far from perfect, you're the one they can rely on, the one who can handle it. You're the one who wants to help. That's you!

I treasure every lonely moment in my life. I treasure every time I've been verbally attacked, bullied, treated unfairly, had my heart broken, had my spirit broken. I've survived being left to fend for myself. It's given my heart such beauty and wings to fly. It is nice helping to protect others. Now I can be someone's peaceful moment.

Looking back, I see God's grace. I see that God's loving hand has always been there. I also see that God has brought out the beauty in me through all I have been through. The times I felt alone and like I didn't have protection strengthened me. I learned how to stand up for myself and others.

If you can be alone and happy, you can be with someone and be happy. Being married, or in a relationship doesn't make you a clone of someone. You will still be alone at times or lonely at times, or in need of something that your partner isn't giving you. So, you need to be able to give yourself what you need. Be self-sufficient always and let company complement the happiness that already exists within you.

You won't be so happy just because you are married or have money. You can't just push this happy button one day. You have to enjoy your daily life, the times you walk alone. You have to love your mind, your heart's meditations. Then, and only then, will you enjoy the gifts that God has for you.

Being single is just feeling the way you do before you fall in love. Anticipation is delicious.

Some people think their biggest problem is not having someone to love, but we always have someone to love. Love yourself and be kind to yourself. Enjoy watching your growth and happiness. Enjoy seeing yourself blossom.

If you're not in a romantic relationship, then your passion and love are being bottled up for a special meeting of hearts. You have something to look forward to. The best thing about being single is the anticipation of that first look, that first kiss, that first time your heart stops and you lose your breath, the first time you are with someone and feel like you're floating when you're in their arms. Anticipate all that you want and you will get it.

I feel like Miss President today. My spirit is powerful and I am beaming, smiling, on fire. I could walk into a crowded room all by myself and sit in a corner alone feeling complete. Those moments when you want for nothing and realize you have everything are the best moments. All I need is a red dress, a glass of wine, and a beautiful summer night...

Yes I love company, but I have learned to enjoy my own company. So, I can have a good time in my own space and admire my good qualities and embrace my downfalls.

I do not think that we leave the world the same way that we come into it. We come into the world alone, as individuals. We leave the world with the people we love. We become one with our mates and our family and that changes us forever. We are never alone after that.

Everything is an illusion, even loneliness. You're not alone, stop believing that. You are connected to everyone and everything. Get connected! The longer you live, the more people you will be connected with. You are a part of a big family. We are all connected to each other and to nature. When you start to realize that, you will never be alone.

Stop trying to get married and enjoy time to walk with God without distractions. If you're married, stop trying to be single, love your mate. If you have children, get your youth back and repair your childhood by being good to them, by being a big part of their happiness. Be faithful in the blessings you have. Be appreciative and thankful by taking care of your blessings!

Many think being in a relationship defines you. Instead, it is the relationship you have with God, with others, and with the Earth. **How do you treat your mother, brother, sister?** How do you treat our planet? When everyone around you is doing something that violates your inner code of conduct, do you do the same? Are you strong enough to stand up for what you believe in? These are the things that define us.

BEAUTY

"PRETTY FADES BUT BEAUTY STAYS! WHEN YOU ARE BEAUTIFUL, PEOPLE WILL ALWAYS SEEK YOUR PRESENCE BECAUSE BEAUTY SHINES FROM THE SOUL AND HAS ROOTS IN THE HEART."

Deep beauty is like deep waters, you can swim in it, not just look at it. It can cleanse your soul, move your heart, and strengthen your faith. When you see someone who is truly beautiful, it reminds you that there is definitely a creator, because that's the closest thing you will see to an angel walking on earth.

Beauty starts in the heart. When you see someone that has the kind of deep beauty that can just knock you over when you are in their presence, it is a Godly beauty. Pretty may only be on the outside but beauty is a whole new ballpark. The only way you can be beautiful is if you are walking in wisdom, love and understanding.

We live in a world that celebrates the outside of a woman but all the beautiful women I know have hearts of gold and strength of soul. When someone can smile at you and mean it, that is beautiful. When someone is sincere and honest, they will make you triple take! We like pretty but beauty is something we love! You can buy pretty but you cannot buy beauty!

You show me your smooth talk, your outward beauty, your nice car, your big house and I will show you kindness, depth of heart and love. The outside of the cup being beautiful doesn't mean anything unless the inside is filled.

Concentrate on filling your spirit and heart. That will take you much further than a pretty outward appearance. Fill your cup with beauty so that when people pick you up, they can see that you have substance.

When someone is happy, now that is beautiful!

When you are just looking for that brand name piece of clothing, that new car, that nose that everyone will like, you have gotten away from your true self. There is nothing wrong with getting a nose job, with having a new car. The problem comes when these things define you. Don't let pretty get the best of you, be beautiful because of who you are. When you are growing as a person, you become happier and when you are happy, you have a beauty about you that cannot be bought or duplicated.

There is a day for everyone when the "you're pretty" or "you're handsome" days slow down. Hopefully, by that time people love you, know you in so many other ways, and know how beautiful your personality is. God gave us pretty when we didn't have much else, but that should change. As the outer beauty fades, the inner beauty shines like the sun. Then we know what beauty really is.

I saw a vision of myself gray and beautiful. There is a deeper beauty, one that is so powerful, it could move a kingdom. When your heart and soul are beautiful, people will see you and stop and stare at you. There is nothing like a beautiful soul. You can feel and be beautiful at any age.

Femininity is a beautiful thing. I like to feel that soft gentleness that comes with being a woman. In today's world, it is hard to enjoy that. As a woman, I need to constantly have my guard up and protect my emotional

vulnerability. But sometimes I just want to be vulnerable, sweet, and gentle. I want to celebrate the more delicate creature that I am.

I am a woman. I don't need to be equal or just as good as a man. I am different and that is what makes me beautiful. A flower doesn't try to be like a tree because there is something so beautiful, delicate and special about a flower. Why do we need to compare the two? I think we lose the beauty of femininity when we try to make everybody the same.

We focus so much on a man and a woman being equal when really, we are not equal at all. A man is not better than a woman and a woman is not better than a man. Femininity is beautiful. It feels good to have an opinion and my own drive for success and to still maintain the delicate part of me. When we start comparing the sexes we lose the feminine beauty that makes being a woman so special. I like when a guy opens a door for me but only when he respects my opinion, my voice and my choices. I can be a strong woman and still be the beautiful, feminine me.

Every woman has a place where she is safe and peaceful. We all have a soft and delicate beauty about us regardless of how strong we are and how much we fight. We all desire that forehead kiss; we all desire to be held. If a woman lets you into this garden of vulnerability, that is a haven in this world. The beauty behind a woman's smile could heal the world. Deep in a woman's heart there is a lot of love. It could take your breath away and change your life if you let a woman be her delicate self around you.

Every woman has a unique beauty of her own. When a woman feels safe enough, she will open up and show it to you. When a woman feels loved, she will smile and be beautiful around you.

LOVE

"LOVE GIVES LIFE COLOR. MAY I ALWAYS BE COLORED WITH LOVE."

Giving love is like having a child. Once it goes beyond you, it is not yours any longer. Love has its own wings, so let it fly away. Love gives your heart legs and trusting that it is from God, you will let it walk away. Let the love you give do its work. God is love so have faith in love, give it freely. How can you get hurt by showing love unless you don't have faith in it?

We all struggle with this, especially when we have feelings for someone, or even love them. It is natural to want your love to be returned to you but that isn't the reason you give it. Once you understand that, it will be so much easier to love. There is no reason to let your heart ache because you love someone or you gave someone love. Love without expectations. Love that is free is the best love there is. When we give love freely, we are showing faith in love and, so, giving it to God. Giving love and regretting it is not what love is about. Love isn't selfish and doesn't seek its own needs. Love doesn't get angry with someone if they don't return it, or return it right when we want them to. Trust that God is love so when we love, we are doing something very spiritual. When we love, we are sending out powerful vibrations into the universe. When we show and give love, we are sending out healing to that person, or people, or to the world. Be happy and feel good about loving someone and showing it! Don't fight loving someone. Love isn't meant to be fought. Feel that love and set it free.

If it isn't real, what is it for? People treat love like a cold, like it's something you can just catch. If it doesn't make you want to be a better person, or if it's not more than timing, what is it for? It is time for you to discover love? You're going to be swept off your feet, but for real.

You want someone by your side who builds you up, not someone who destroys you. Love is a beautiful thing so don't settle for the imitation. Marvin Gaye was right when he said, "Ain't nothing like the real thing, baby." I've become very patient. Don't settle, never settle. Wait until your heart is inclined. When it is, don't let someone settle for you.

Love is just and wise.

Love is the strongest force in the universe. Love can make you fight for something. Love can make you walk out that door and go to work. Love can make your heart smile. Love can also be stern and have boundaries if it needs to. Love will make you teach your child how to behave and love will make you tell them no at times. Love will make you tell your partner that the way they are acting or a decision they have made is not the best way. Love is strong enough to look out for the greater good.

Love is when you want to walk down the aisle with someone and keep on that same walk forever. Love is when you're excited from the first moment you see someone and that excitement never fades. You're no longer in want or need because someone has filled that space in your heart. Your want and need is standing right in front of you. Yes, I want you.

When you love someone it isn't a passing feeling. Lust or passion can come and go for someone. Love is constant and strong. When you love someone you will want to spend your life with them. Love is looking into someone's eyes and seeing your past, present and future all wrapped up into one.

Love is the best and only foundation for a marriage. It isn't advisable to get married because you are impatient for a family. It isn't prudent to get married because you don't want to be alone. It isn't shrewd to want someone so badly that you do not care if they truly love you or not. Many marriages fail because the two people in it don't truly love each other. Love is the most plentiful ingredient in a good marriage.

I think a man's role in the family is to add emotional stability. Every woman wants to be loved and every child wants a dad to pat them on the back. A man that loves his family will help the wife feel valued and be a source of emotional strength for his family. A man's love is needed.

I say this because everyone makes the man the hunter. Many men think if they provide financially for their family, that's all they need to do. When a child grows up, they rarely tell their parents thank you for the clothing you bought me for school, even though those things are important. They remember the love and it's the love that shapes them and helps them show love to others. A child can grow up in a home with a mother's love but without the father's love, that child will be missing something.

Every child needs the encouragement and the love of a father. A girl learns how to be loved and what kind of man she should marry from the love she receives from her father. A boy learns how to show love as a male in the family from his father. If the father verbally or physically abuses the mother, this will cause a son to think that is how he should show love to women. A father's love adds emotional stability to the family.

Knowledge puffs up; love builds up. We can go to the moon, make a computer and surf the Internet, but everyone isn't well feed. We are such a smart society, yet we're missing the more important things.

People think that our technology is something to brag about, but looking at the state of humanity, it definitely is not. We need to put more of our energy into showing love to each other. We give money for missiles, technology, bigger homes and many times miss out on giving money for the good of people. If we choose love, we will notice the real needs of our communities and the world, and meet those needs.

If you want to be held, you have to know how to hold somebody. If you want to be swept off your feet, you have to be willing to take your feet off the ground. If you want to gain love, you have to give it.

For everything we want, there is a sacrifice. If you really want to be loved, you have to give love. You have to go through the ups and downs of a relationship. Go through that unsure time when you don't know if someone feels the same. This is hard for many. If you want someone to love you and always be there for you, you have to be there for them. We can all make a list of what we want in a partner or what kind of relationship we want to have. We do play a significant role in that. Anything you want, you have to be willing to give. You also need to be willing to risk heartbreak, or just be on the roller coaster of love to experience it.

There is no need to force love, to find love, or to wait for love. It is the strongest force in the universe, it will find you! Love will hunt you down and take hold of your soul for good. Love will put you in the sweetest submission.

Love can start a war, end a fight and heal the world. You don't need to look for love, love will come for you. When it does, it will make you obedient to it, it will knock you to your knees. You don't have to convince love, love will convince you.

When you fall in love, you give away a part of yourself that is tied to someone else. Think of love as tying a bow, putting a rope together, or locking a door. Love is a joining together. There is no love where God is not involved, so now, it is that much stronger. Be careful what you wish for, it will find you alright. You will never be the same after real love hits you.

I'd rather have a man who loves me and is generous with me than a rich man any day. A man who truly loves me will always take care of me and I will take care of him. I would like a man rich in spirit. That would make me a truly rich woman.

A man that has money can truly love a woman. But love isn't about things. You have to love someone with or without what they have. It's not the things that make a man. A man who puts love first, will always be rich in every way. If a man has a lot of money or things, that can be taken away in an instant. So, I'd rather be with a man who is generous with me in love and who would share his last dollar with me, instead of one who would hold back millions from me. I want a man rich in heart. Let his heart be bigger than his pockets. That is the depth I want.

Cupid keeps challenging me. I battle with cupid every Valentine's Day. I seem to think that love is greater than Valentine's Day, or the holiday we make it to be. The display of this or that pales in comparison to true love, and the desire that needs no one to witness it or to validate it but God.

You can say thank you, pull out chairs, or make a candlelit dinner any day of the week. You can show up with flowers, make the bed, or smile at the one you love just because you want to. In the thick of this world, love should make things better. We can say we love someone, or we can actually love daily. Love is something we do year round.

There is an initial feeling you get when you meet someone who you could be more with. This feeling can hit you, or even slap you in the face. Rose-colored glasses are worn by many. After you wear them, it's very important to take them off so you can see.

Let love take it's time with you. There is no need to rush love. Just let it be, it will be what it's going to be. In time, all things are revealed. So take your time. Don't control it, or feel the need to define it. First wait and see what it is.

Wind, how do you hold it? You don't; you let it move you. A woman, how do you handle her? You don't; you love her and treat her with tenderness. You treat her like a precious gift.

Women want to feel appreciated! Let the woman in your life know you appreciate her. It's the little things you do to show that! Tell the woman in your life that you love her. Make sure she knows by the way you treat her. If you are kind and treat a good woman with tenderness, you will have satisfaction that is way better than riches and glory.

Love will make you stop and think about what you're going to say to someone. Love will make you stick up for someone. Love will make you brave. Love is strong enough to make your fears fade. Love is lasting, it won't break.

The love of your other half doesn't have a beginning or an end. You have always been connected with them, and you always will be. You can always feel that presence. Be on the frequency of the love of your life, you will always find them in your heart and mind.

Be proud of yourself when you can put yourself out there to love. A heart that is willing to love will find love. So, when you notice that you love big, get ready because you will have a great big love story to match it!

Love is not a weakness, it is a great strength. Exposing yourself to love and its power can be scary. So, if you're one of those people who love and love hard, don't feel bad about that. Having the capacity to love is the greatest treasure.

Love isn't a high or low feeling; it is steady and sure. Love isn't based on certain conditions. The sky doesn't disappear in the storm or in darkness, it is continuously there through all weather conditions and it keeps functioning. Love isn't something you can give away and take back. If it's love, it just is. If you really love someone then you can't lose that love, so you set it free.

Like children, when we are learning love we first take baby steps in it. We get so caught up in what we want and the magic of love, that we expect it to fulfill our needs. We cry out to it and ask it to feed us. As we grow up in love, we learn how to give love. We don't walk around love's playground and say, "It's mine." Grown love knows how to give it and let it go do what it's going to do!

Trust me in this, we all have relationship issues. All the couples I know that love each other have serious issues. Falling for someone is fun and magical. Continuing with someone for a lifetime can drive you almost crazy but be the most rewarding thing in your life. So don't think there is something wrong with you because there is something wrong with everyone. I'm so wrong sometimes that I'm right.

A friend asked a good question, "What does a woman need most from a man in a relationship?" It's simple: Love. That goes beyond attraction, sex, or agreement. Women want to know that they're loved for more than how they look and in spite of some of the crazy things we do. All women have emotionally unstable times at least once a month. When a woman feels loved, she tends to start to act right because she feels safe and has no need to test you. There are no perfect women, but when you love a woman for her imperfections as much as the things you like about her, she will become perfect for you.

Men are not as emotionally strong as they may seem. Sometimes women think they can say things or do things to men and that it doesn't faze them, but it does. A man may not call a woman and freak out or cry to her, but they get hurt, too. Men have insecurities; they just deal with them differently. They may not call because they don't know what to say, or they may stay away because they are waiting for a better time to approach a subject. Men can't always be the protectors. Sometimes, they are dealing with things that make them withdraw. We need to give guys a break sometimes, too. Women tend to interpret things too quickly into a man not caring about her, when in actuality he may be afraid to say he doesn't know what to do or how to do it.

If I gave a baby a check for a million dollars, that baby would chew on it and tear it up. If I gave a child an expensive piece of art, they would play with it and break it. So why do you give yourself away to fools when you are priceless? Bring yourself before a person with a heart that is worthy of you. Give yourself to someone who reflects appreciation and love in their eyes for you.

You may want someone really bad, you may even love them, but that isn't a good enough reason to give yourself to them. It's difficult to handle heartbreak or a normal obsession over someone you care for deeply. Still, you must separate yourself from foolish choices in love. A foolish choice is when you enter into love with so much to give and not being appreciated for it. If you were a skilled lawyer and I asked you to work for my law firm for $2 an hour, you would say 'No.' What if you really loved my company, would that change your mind? No, it wouldn't. No matter how much you loved my company, you wouldn't accept an offer that showed complete lack of appreciation for your skill. You would laugh at me. Now think of love as a binding agreement that lasts longer than any business deal you could make. When you think of it that way, isn't it important to have a partner who can offer you more than two-dollar love? Look for a partner who can offer you love that is priceless and love that is so good.

There is beauty in a soft approach and words that are pleasant.

Love will make you treat someone with kindness. Sometimes a whisper is so much better than a shout.

I found someone to love. I found someone who needed to be cared for and adored. I found someone who needed a hug. I found someone who had no idea what beauty was locked inside of her. One day, I finally found me.

So many keep looking for someone to make them whole and that is an endless search of self. You are the love of your life. Everything and everyone is becoming an extension of you. The person that you've been searching for and dying to meet is you. The person, who can make you smile and glow all day long is you. The person you've been waiting to be in awe of and to give your heart, body and soul to is you. When you find that person, you will know that it's love.

We need to be kind and empathetic to each other. There is so much pain and sorrow because of the lack of love that some show. The heroes of this world know how to connect with people. The true leaders of this world, who carry us, know how to give of themselves, because they have a strong relationship with God. It feels so good to transfer tenderness to someone emotionally and mentally.

Lovingly put your hand on someone's shoulder and reassure them that you care for them and that everything is going to be alright. Hold someone when they are down and let them cry on your shoulder. It will be the most rewarding thing you could ever do. It will make life worth living. I love, therefore, I give and live. I am so thankful for the greatest gift in the world, to be able to comfort someone, to truly love others is a gift.

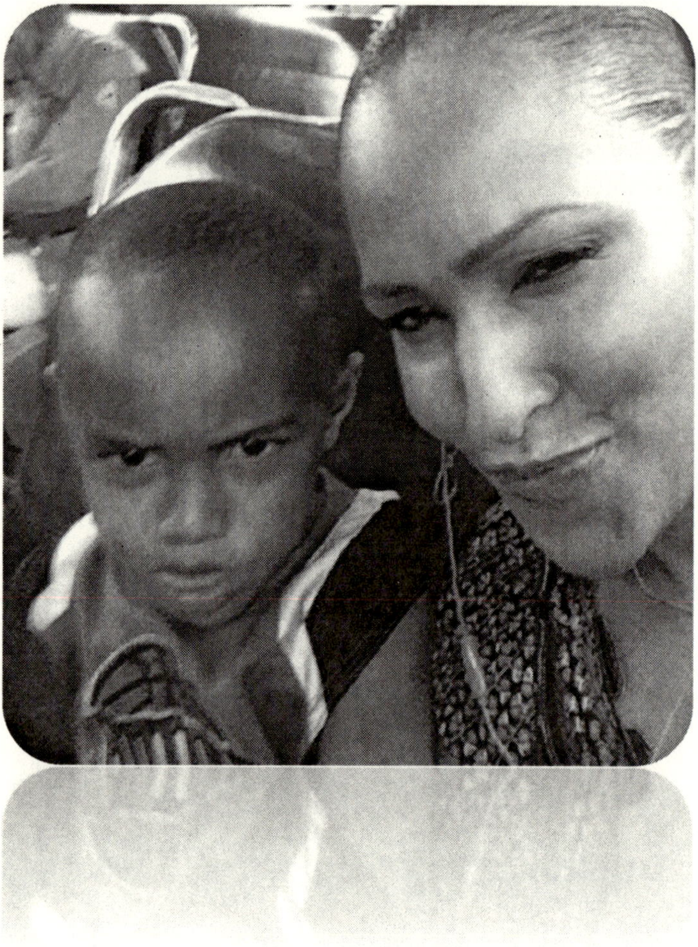

GIVING

"MY LIFE IS AS GOOD AS THE PEOPLE I AFFECT IN IT, THE LIVES I TOUCH ... LIFE IS WORTH LIVING WHEN YOU LEARN THE GIFT OF GIVING!"

Giving creates a circle. When we give, that giving keeps going until it comes back to us. We don't give so that we receive, but it still puts us in the circle of giving. When you are in this circle of giving, you are in the circle of success because everything we have in life is given to us and is a gift. It doesn't matter how hard we work, we are still given things everyday that we cannot work for. Life is about appreciating what we have, and by giving we show this. We also bring more good things to ourselves. So, when we give, we become a part of the giving circle.

Everything in the world gets taken care of through giving. When your child needs food, you give to them from what you have been given. Love for others makes us want to take care of each other. When you walk by someone or see someone who needs food, how are they going to get food? Yes, everyone should work and take care of themselves and their family, but we are all an extended family. So if no one reaches out and gives that person something to eat, how will they eat? Yes, if you believe in God, you have faith and know that God supplies all things for others. We have been given a chance to help supply each other's needs when we are willing to give.

The golden rule is to do unto others as you would have them do unto you.

If you were drowning in water, would you want someone to help you? If you wanted to go out for an evening, but you didn't have anywhere to go, or the money to just go out alone, wouldn't you want someone to treat you to a nice evening? All of us can answer 'Yes' to that when we put our egos aside. Giving is really doing unto others as you would have them do unto you.

There is a deep spiritual satisfaction from giving because when we give we are working on the highest spiritual plane. Our bodies become healthier and happier. If you want to live long, keep giving. This is a way to draw closer to God, or to what many like to call the universe. When you do this it gives you a great deal of peace and tranquility. When we give, it increases our own happiness and that of others. When we give, it contributes greatly to our own spirituality and that of the world's.

I write things and many times I look back and wonder where it came from. I wonder where it came from so quickly and poetically with a message in it that even I may not have discovered until it came out. It reminds me of how magnificent God is. We all have gifts and these gifts do not belong to us.

Whatever gift you have does not belong to you. When you hold back your love for life, you take it away from the world. If you can sing, if you have a beautiful voice, it was meant to be heard. You could be great at fixing things, and so you were meant to fix things for others, not just yourself. When we get so caught up in what we can get from giving, we lose the real joy of giving. When it's all about how much money we can get, we don't enjoy life. The joy in life is from having a purpose and we all have something to give to the world.

Today is a good day to do something for someone else. Give somebody a smile, a handshake, or a dollar. Take somebody to their favorite place to eat or make somebody something to eat.

You don't have to be Bill Gates to give. You don't have to give someone a home to make someone feel at home with you. All the little things we do daily add up to great big things. If all you can do is share with someone, then do that. Someone may need a ride to work and if you have a car, you may be able to help them. Many times we tell ourselves when we get everything we think we need, we will be able to give. We forget that everything we have we are constantly receiving. You don't own anything; you're just borrowing it or holding onto it to let it go.

When you see people, *really* look at them. When you walk by that homeless guy, smile and say hello. When you walk by the janitor, give him a cupcake. Whatever you have, share it. Jesus fed a crowd of people with a basket of fish. When we share, there is always more. In the Bible, God fed people with manna from heaven. They were directed not to save it. Not saving the manna in the wilderness was important. Many save things all their lives and leave them behind when they die. Stop worrying constantly about tomorrow and share today!

The best way to get out of your own despair is to share.

You can waste the whole day being depressed and worrying about anything and everything, or you can give to others. While you are praying, pray for someone else, too.

RELIGION

"MY LIFELONG QUESTION FOR GOD HAS BEEN ASNSWERED. THE ANSWER IS THAT I AM NOT ALWAYS GOING TO GET THE ANSWER. I WILL NOT ALWAYS UNDERSTAND EVERYTHING, THAT'S WHY FAITH IS SO IMPORTANT."

I pray for tolerance. You don't have to think like me or be like me to be liked by me, or even loved! I pray for soundness of mind. I want my mind to constantly be in a positive place and a logical place regardless of what is going on around me. I pray for courage. I pray that I may continue to conquer and step out on faith. I pray for joy, that my smile may stay vibrant and heartfelt!

I will not exclude you because you look different than me. I invite all to be a part of my friend circle. That is what love says.

I had this idea that I needed to know how things were going to turn out.

I was upset that when I prayed God didn't just say, do exactly this. Then, I finally got it one day. Life is about the freedom we were given to make our own choices. That is a gift we don't always understand and we are not always able to use correctly. Principles should always guide our decisions. It is fear that causes us to want someone to tell us exactly what to do. It is fear that makes us not want to take responsibility for our own lives. It's like we need someone to blame when something doesn't work out. The truth is, when you get over that fear, you start living in the power to make the right choices. You can actually make choices that make you happy. You can make choices that you are proud of. Stop being afraid to take responsibility for your life, and I promise you, you will start living.

The question isn't, 'Why does God allow people to suffer?' The question is, 'Why do humans harm other humans?' The question is not, 'Why doesn't God feed the world?' The question is, 'Why do we not share with each other all over the world?' The question isn't, 'Why does religion cause war and separation?' The question is, 'Why people do what they do?' God has the answers but do we answer to love? Do we?

I used to pray to God and be upset, asking 'Why? Why do you let these things happen?' That was a question filled with my own stupidity and lack of knowledge. God has made a beautiful world and people in it. God made animals and oceans. God made love and kindness. So the real question is, 'Why do we as a people destroy each other and the Earth?' We always have a choice. God gave us free will and we should use it for good.

In your mind stay in the place you want to be and you will see your blessings show up. Faith calls blessings and blessings answer to faith. Before you even asked for it, it was already on its way to you. You just figured it out but it was already figured out. You just asked but it has already been given... You don't belong in sorrow so don't stay there. Start with your attitude and be happy now!

Now is the time to embrace joy, love and happiness! You have been given so many gifts and blessings and you may not have noticed all of them. Your mind is you, so think about all your blessings and concentrate on the things you want and be where you want to be now.

Among those that are materially rich, there is an attitude that perhaps you can buy your way past God and the importance of spirituality in your life. Then, among the very poor there is an attitude that God isn't there and that perhaps they are alone. Neither is true. You cannot escape God because God made you, your connection with God is essential to your happiness. (Psalm 139:7-14)

Regardless of who you are, or where you are from, you have a yearning for spirituality. We need God like we need air. That is exactly why people have always made up a religion or a god to serve because we have an inner rule book. We are born with a conscience that tells us that certain things are wrong and that certain things are right.

"You chart the path ahead of me and tell me where to stop and rest. Every moment you know where I am." (Psalm 39:3) There is a time for everything. (Ecclesiastes 3:1)

Take a deep breath, sometimes you need to rest. Be active and productive, not just busy. We all need to pace ourselves! Take time to smile, eat and love your family. Take time to pray. We all need balance in our lives.

But the fruit of the Spirit is love, joy, peace, forbearance, kindness, goodness, faithfulness. (Galatians 5:22)

I remember that if I am walking by faith and not by sight, then I am being fruitful in these things. I fall down but I get up and keep trying to walk by faith.

"Pure and genuine religion in the sight of God the Father means caring for orphans and widows in their distress and refusing to let the world corrupt you." (James 1:27)

Be honest and try to make the world a better place! That is the best way to serve God. Look after those who cannot defend themselves. Look after those who need help and assistance. We can all say that we love God, but those who love God will show it by the way they treat people. We show it in the compassion that we extend to everyone.

"Consider it pure joy, whenever you face trials of many kinds, because you know that the testing of your faith produces perseverance." (James 1:2, 3)

Trials make us stronger and help us develop the qualities that truly make us grow. Growth can feel painful and uncomfortable. You will face times of darkness and confusion but through all that, you will grow in ways you didn't realize you could. God's goal for you is not so that you can look beautiful and rich. God wants you to actually be rich in spirit and beautiful in your mind and heart. God wants everlasting treasures to be yours.

Jonah was afraid and ran away from God. He climbed down into the dark hold of a ship to hide there from God. (Jonah Chapter 1)

Many times we try to hide and, thankfully, God finds us. No matter how dark or deep we go, God can find us and help us. Jonah tried to run as many of us do. You can run and hide in alcohol, drugs, depression, and anything that can keep you from facing life, but God will find you. That isn't a threat, it's a gift.

The truth isn't afraid to be questioned...

You are not bad for asking questions. I don't care what people say, everyone has questions. If you don't understand what everyone believes is true, that doesn't make you bad. Chances are many have the same questions you do, and they are just afraid to ask.

What is all this I hear about when God comes they will get what they deserve?

Love doesn't think like this...Revenge and hatred are not from God. This need to punish and harm is a human sickness.

"Timely advice is as lovely as golden apples in a silver basket." (Proverb 24:11)

Timing is everything. Sometimes it is better to let go all together, until another time. Just because you want something now, doesn't mean it is the time for you to get it.

Man has dominated man to his own injury, as Ecclesiastes 8:9 says. Then we foolishly blame God. As Proverb says, wisdom cries in the streets, but who will listen?

Love takes so much less effort and peace feels so much better. The Earth is our home; only a fool destroys their own home. Only a fool puts their fate in the hand of another who doesn't care or know how to save.

"Then the Jewish leaders sought to arrest him; but no hand was laid on him, for God's time had not yet come." (John 7:30)

Do not be afraid of man. People can only do what God allows them to do. You will escape from the hands of many for doing the right thing!

People will act ugly and may be unkind at times. You keep your smile. You keep the rhythmic energy of joy that flows through you. You keep your stance and know that people may act wrong when you do right, but they will come around because God will lift you up. If you humble yourself, you will be exalted, and if you exalt yourself you, will be humbled. Forgive, give, love and be the lion or lioness you are for what's right!

I am running in a way that I may win the prize. (1 Corinthians 9:24-27)

Paul said that he had to beat his body and lead it as a slave. He was really saying that he had to discipline himself. You can waste your day complaining, or you can do the things that will make you feel better about yourself. Go for the win!

Living life sober can bring you real happiness. Being disciplined is actually freeing to the body, mind and spirit. By recognizing your spiritual, emotional and physical needs, you will be less attracted to simply going after wants. We all yearn to live better lives. It takes effort and discipline to accomplish things. Start living life sober by doing the work that brings greater satisfaction then just doing what you feel.

Jesus said, "You go on, and I'll come later when it is the right time." (John 7:8)

When the brothers of Jesus urged him to show up and show out, Jesus declined! He said that he would come at the right time. You don't have to jump because someone wants you to.

It has already worked out, the impossible is possible, amazing is always available, incredible is credible, love is the way, exciting is your life! Happiness is in the attitude you show! Blessed means thankful and giving is the greatest joy! Your cup is overflowing because God is filling it. You're not alone and rich is in the spirit you show!

Sometimes you need a miracle. Sometimes only a miracle can help you and faith sees the miracle before it comes. Faith sees the continual blessings. Faith remembers the miracles of the past and is thankful for all the miracles to come. So, I smile because I am a walking miracle by faith. Joy is in faith because faith always sees the rainbow.

"I cry to God, I call and call to him. Oh, that he would listen. I am in deep trouble and I need his help so badly. All night long I pray, lifting my hands to heaven, pleading. There can be no joy for me until he acts. I think of God and moan, overwhelmed with longing for his help. I cannot sleep until you act. I am too distressed even to pray!" (Psalm 77:1-4)

Perhaps you feel like David did when he wrote this. We all need help. Psalm 139 says that God knows what you're going to say before you even say it. It says that your path is already charted out before you. Have faith and keep walking. You will make it through this and everything will work out even better than you could imagine. If you trust in God, God will act on your part!

"Be swift about hearing, slow about speaking, slow about wrath."(Proverbs 15:28)

Listening is an art to be mastered. It is very important when you wish to teach or preach a message that you know your audience. You may assume someone is a certain way or has no spiritual knowledge. Find out so you can touch their heart. Knowledge can be so powerful when spoken through wisdom. If you really listen to someone, you will be able to speak to them in a way that can touch the heart.

I grew up in the hood, the Bible hood. That's what church can be. Guns don't kill people, people kill people. The Bible doesn't cut you but people can use it to do that. I'm not afraid of the Bible, I'm afraid of who's holding it. I've already been cut up, I'm not afraid. I know how to use my sword, too, so come on with it!

Many times people can use religion and the Bible to make it okay to treat others badly or to judge. I learned the Bible well as a youth and I consider that a great gift. I grew in wisdom and love by reading and learning about the Bible. I don't let religious people scare me because my knowledge of the scriptures protects me from that.

It is very good to go to a religious place of meeting; I recommend choosing wisely and daily studying and reading the Bible yourself.

"Peter got down out of the boat walked on the water and came toward Jesus. But when he saw the wind, he was afraid and beginning to sink, cried out, "Lord, save me!" Immediately Jesus reached out his hand and caught him. "You of little faith," he said, "why did you doubt?"(Matthew 14:29-31)

When we doubt we start to sink. Peter was fine walking on water until he started to question himself and God's ability to help him do something miraculous. There was still a hand to help him get back up. There is always a hand to help you when you start to sink.

You know what I love most about the account of Jesus? Jesus sat with the sinners, the people that everyone else had condemned. Jesus showed compassion to those that were sick; he fed crowds.

If it is up to the history or current acts of Christianity, then not many are going to be attracted to it. Christians should be so attractive, not high and mighty and judgmental. Jesus' message was also not just to scare people into serving God. We are not being Christians when people think they are going to hell or that we think that is where they are going.

We are not doing our job when they think God is vengeful, a mystery, and that God is only at our house. We should show love to people. We should protect and care for each other and show compassion to others.

Mathew 5:46 asks us what good we are doing if we only love those who love us.

The Gospel says to widen out in your love. If we only love those who love us, we are doing what everyone else does.

I will not be so consumed with what I want today. I will be an observer of creation. I will look outside of my limited mind, limited love and limited wisdom. I will tap into the source of unlimited wisdom, unlimited love and unlimited power. I will rise up, see beyond and feel the magic of life.

If I live out of my wisdom alone, then I know nothing. If I show my love only, I am limited in my love. If I operate from my power only, I will not have enough power to see the magic of life. If I walk with God daily and tap into God's love, it will teach me God's wisdom. It will guide me and God's power will allow me to do anything and everything. When I connect with God, I connect with everyone and everything.

Everything that is good about me comes from God. God is the author of the good in my life.

I am only on fire and full of courage because of my faith in the Creator. You know why I walk up to my opponents without fear? Not because I can take anybody, but because the one who is with me is greater than anyone who could be against me.

Neither do people light a lamp and put it under a bowl. Instead they put it on its stand, and it gives light to everyone in the house. (Matthew 5:15)

If you can be a lighthouse, pick yourselves up and do it! The world needs you! People need your love and your light. Use your life experience; even the things that were difficult to make it through, and use it to help others. You are strong. Let your faith strengthen others!

"It is better to live in the corner of an attic than to live in a mansion with a cranky woman! (Proverb 21:9) "Better a meal of vegetables where there is love than a fattened calf with hatred." (Prov. 15:17)

So true! It is better to be around people who build you up instead of tearing you down! Proverbs says that only a foolish man tears down his own household! Don't be a fool...I pity the fools!

Seek the association of those who do not crush your spirit and those who know love.

"These men were very jealous of Joseph and sold him to be a slave in Egypt. But God was with him and gave him favor and unusual wisdom, so that Pharaoh appointed him in charge of the affairs of the palace."(Acts 7:9-14)

Joseph's brothers rejected him, but God gave him favor and he was used to save the very ones that rejected him. God's favor can take you way farther than man's favor!

"But our fathers rejected Moses and wanted to return to Egypt." They said, "For we don't know what has become of this Moses."(Acts 7:39,40)

When we run in a hurry to get ahead by our own means, many times we are really returning back and making our journey longer and harder. You've got to do it the right way. The wrong way will only take you in the wrong direction.

A detour is a deviation from a direct course of action. On our road to faith, let us take the direct route. Faith stays the course instead of making its own way.

Matthew 19:5,6 says that God created man and woman, and that a man should leave his father and mother and stick to his wife forever, that the two would become one and what God has joined together, no one can put apart.

Today people try to go in and out of relationships, but when you are in a relationship God has put together, you cannot sever that, even by leaving. When a soul is joined to a soul, it will always be.

"You have turned on my light! The Lord my God has made my darkness turn to light." (Psalm 19:28)

Your darkness has already been turned into light today. You are walking in the light of day.

In Matthew 8:8 the army officer said, "If you will only stand here and say, 'Be healed,' my servant will get well!"

In this account, Jesus was amazed at this man's faith! Faith is essential to approaching God. When we show faith, we say a prayer, and after we ask for it or pray about it, we are no longer concerned with it. I remember when Hannah prayed for Samuel, she was crying bitterly and in deep anguish. After she prayed, she started eating again and the scriptures say she was happy. When we have faith, we let go and let God as the saying goes!

Psalm 135:1-3 says that it is wonderful and pleasant to live in harmony with each other. It compares harmony to holiness. To live together in harmony means peace for all.

The call goes out for us to live in harmony with each other. The call goes out for peace. May there be peace among us. May we learn love and teach it to each other. Love is big and wide including all people. Love has no beginning and no end, it goes on forever. Love reaches outside of its own community and household. Love reaches far to the distant parts of the Earth. Love causes the sun to rise and keeps it at the right distance from the Earth so that is warms us.

In Proverbs 12:4 it says that a worthy wife is a crown to her husband but that the other kind corrodes his strength and brings down all that he does.

If you love a good woman, she will devote her life to you. She will be your biggest fan and give you a helping hand throughout your life. The other kind will bring you so much stress. I love that, the other kind. We know what kind that is. It's important to choose a woman who loves you for who you are, not for what you have. It's important to pick a woman who checks how her heart looks more than how her hair looks. Let your favor be with a woman who speaks to you in such a way to make you better. Proverb Chapter 31 says that a good woman will be praised and her husband will say that although there are many fine women, that she is better than all of them to him.

Romans 12:9 says to cling to what is good.

You can do this, you can do everything. There isn't one thing that could happen to you that you are not built or made to handle and conquer. You were made in the most powerful image of all; you were made in God's image. Cling to what is good, yes, cling to the extraordinary, cling to miracles and cling to joy.

Promotion and power do not come from Earth but only from God as Psalm 75:1 declares.

I am feeling very thankful because I have been blessed greatly. But this is the message I have in my spirit: "There will be more and even greater blessings."

We need to stop learning about good things and leaving them with the groups we learned them in, just so we can go back and act nice next Sunday. We need to stop reading books that have no value past the time we've read them. Stop talking about what needs to be done and start doing it and living it.

The tides are changing. Return to doing better things. We yearn for a better world. We want it so bad that we can taste it. When you get that taste, go with it! Connect with God, the Earth, and every human being. Let kindness become common again. Let's allow the law of love to reign. It isn't working to be selfish and to harm each other. Will somebody tell that to each new generation? It's as if history has taught us nothing. We act like we are trying a new thing when we are doing the same thing over and over again. Let's break from the madness and start living right. We need to change for our survival.

It's time for everyone to be humanitarian! We help each other, that is how we grow. If other people aren't eating, we care. If other people are living in poverty, we fight to help them. No matter how they got there. We cannot have a world worth living in unless we care for it and care for each other. We are reaching the humanitarian age.

FRIENDSHIP

"A FRIEND IS SOMEONE WHO WILL BRING YOU AN UMBRELLA WHEN YOU ARE IN THE RAIN. A FRIEND WILL GIVE YOU A COLD CUP OF WATER TO COOL YOU OFF IN THE HEAT OF LIFE."

I am weak, therefore, I am strong. I am willing to see my flaws. I say what I think and feel so I don't sound perfect. You may think I'm wrong or foolish at times and that is good because I am. But if you want to, walk with me and watch me fall. I'll get up and it might just be because you gave me a hand.

I value all of my friends and family. I value all the help I have gotten and all that is to come. I am thankful for having some really uplifting friends in my life and I celebrate them!

If I am your friend, you have a good friend. Many are there for the good times. If you go through the not so seemingly good times, I will still be there. If you need an

army to fight for you, take me instead! One good friend is better than many who will scatter quickly in fear. If you have one good friend, you have an army.

Having one good friend is better than having a thousand that are not true friends. Look for quality, not quantity. A good friend is hard to find, so when you find one treasure them. The best way to get a good friend is to be a good friend. Be the kind of friend that someone can count on, be the kind of friend that someone wants to call.

I'm glad my words can comfort you and help you through this time. If you need to hide, I will shield you with my words. If you're feeling cold, I will warm you with the fire of my love. Come now and see me, and I will see you. I will walk by you today. When you want to cry, you can have my shoulder. If your burdens are too much to handle, give me some of them. I will sit with you just so you don't have to sit alone. I will hold your hand. When you sleep, I will scare all the monsters away.

Someone may come along who knows what you're going through. Or someone may come along who tells you exactly what you need to hear. There is someone who cares. There is someone who wants to scare all the monsters away in your life. You have a good friend, and if it's God, well, that's the best friend you can have.

When I am weak, I am powerful in you. Being sick has reminded me of good things. In a very weak state, friends and family have come to my aid and I have seen the love there is for me and that I am valued. Even in sickness, this made me strong. All the concern and calls have been

appreciated. I give love and I am loved. Thank you to all my friends.

When we are weak, friendship can strengthen us and awaken us. When I was weak, my friends made me powerful. Friendship can heal a soul that is sick. Friendship can be the best medicine we can receive.

You are wonderful for all the right reasons. When you laugh the sky lights up. When you come in a room time stops. When you breathe the world feels normal again. When your heart is beating, it is a blessing to everyone you pass. They don't even know that your very being is helping the Earth stand. So, if no one said it yet today, thank you.

I want you to know that you are appreciated. The world doesn't always notice the angels that are in its midst. Do not let this trouble you. Be the loving soul you are because you help the world go round.

Don't wait to be there for me at my funeral, to fly out and come see me when I am gone. Don't wait to say nice things when I am no longer present. Why throw me a party when I cannot stand by you? Say that you love me now. Be there for me now, while I'm breathing.

Many times it isn't until someone is gone that we appreciate them. All of a sudden when they are not around we remember only the good that they did, but when they were alive we may have punished them. Love the people in your lives now, while you can show it to them. Treasure them now, while they can see it and be encouraged by it.

SEXY

"CONFINDENCE IS SEXY! BE CONFIDENTLY YOU... "

Loyalty is sexy, patience is beautiful, hard work is satisfying, and love is a fire that cannot be put out. Humility brings peace, truth is a treasure, and honesty is irresistible! To speak of such things excites me! Good things can bring such contentment. Chase these things and you will be irresistible!

If you want to be sexy, cultivate attractive qualities. We all find peace attractive. We all yearn for commitment and hard work. I haven't seen one person that didn't wear humility and honesty well. These are the things in life that are truly satisfying and will bring others to you.

There is something so sexy about obstacles. Well, since we know they can't stop us and when we get past them, when we conquer them, when we wrestle them right out of our lives, we just look and feel better. I can't explain it but they make me shine brighter.

Let what you have been through in your life make you better. If you are a diamond in the rough, dust yourself off and watch how you shine with your gorgeous self!

Sexy is taking out my own trash after work. Sexy is defending myself. Sexy is not letting anyone tell me who I am. Sexy is not caring what you think of me. Sexy is standing for something and not falling for everything. Sexy is not striving for a picture perfect life, because I'm picture perfect. Sexy is smiling and being joyous all by myself. Sexy is you needing me. Sexy is hugging someone else because I cried those tears.

It is much more attractive to see a woman who knows who she is, than to see a pretty picture. Being sexy isn't about going to dinner and eating a salad. It's sexy to not always care about how you look, and to instead care about how you live. It is sexy to see someone who cares for others and who is strong. Sexy isn't about your skirt, or about how well you wear it. It's about the person that is wearing it!

Sexy is wearing an inexpensive dress that hugs your every curve. Sexy is walking on the beach with no shoes on.

Sexy is acting with confidence. Sexy isn't always on purpose. You will notice that people are looking at you when you least expect it. You may get more compliments when you don't even take the time to dress up. Sexy is wearing jogging pants and still getting attention because it's you.

So, the only thing you can do is renew your strength because you don't lose. You built a city and you must keep up the walls around it. You have your own army and you don't surrender. If someone is going to take you down, they will have to fight for it. That is a win you won't just give into.

When it comes to love and romance, I believe in the struggle for it. A struggle can be very sexy. It's sexy to tell your partner what you think and to not always agree. Honesty in a relationship can be very seductive. When someone challenges you and conquers your heart, it's a very powerful thing. Don't always back down. Stand up and rise to the struggle.

Wisdom brings a beauty to the soul that outshines any outward appearance. Wisdom walking is breathtaking.

The legs of wisdom will turn your head much longer and the eyes of wisdom will capture your heart. The touch of wisdom will give you life. The kiss of wisdom will unravel you and make you fall in a love that is lasting, intensely exciting and fulfilling.

Wisdom is a beautiful and sexy quality in a man or a woman. Someone that is wise will catch your eye and keep your attention. I remember telling a guy I would tackle him mentally and I meant it! Wisdom is captivating. When a man is wise, he can truly touch my heart.

Only intelligent men know how to carry sexy. It's not the level of education; it's the way a man thinks. It's that Daddy quality in a man that I find incredibly sexy. If he can be Daddy then he is mature and knows how to handle himself. I am emotional, impulsive, excitable and fiery. A man who can calm me with intelligence, ah yes, that is sexy. To keep me under some amount of control is enough of a challenge.

When a man is able to deal with me on a level of intelligence, wisdom and with controlled emotions, that makes me feel safe. I don't find a bad boy or as some call it, a rude boy, sexy. It's the strong man who is in control of himself that I find attractive and sexy. It is when his presence sets boundaries. When his presence declares that he is the man in the room. I am not the quiet woman. I speak, I have opinions, and I am competitive. But when a man is a man, I know that I can wear my skirt and be my feminine self. It also lets me know he isn't afraid of my strength or my opinions, that he can handle all of that. There is no need to test the boundaries of a man when those boundaries have already been set from the moment he walks in a room. It's easy to respect him. Now that's something to write about.

A man is sexy when...he has a suit on and unbuttons the top two buttons of his shirt and loosens his tie...When he knows how to grab you and make you blush...When he looks at you and you can't help but smile and look away...When he makes you feel nervous and flustered simply by his presence.

It isn't about the suit or the tie he's wearing; it is about the idea of a man. The power of a man is so moving. When a man looks at you and takes you with his eyes, you can't help but soften. It is about the way he touches you, kisses you, or grabs your waist with such power that it gives you chills. It's when he takes you without saying a word. It's when you get that feeling in your stomach like you're on the dip of a roller coaster, but you're trying so hard to remain cool and you hope he doesn't see it. Just standing close draws you to him. It's everything about him, his arms, the way he breathes, the way he stands when he is all together desirable to you. Now that's the measure of a man.

Sexy is wearing a T-shirt well. Sexy is running bath water and sitting in the steam. Sexy is the way you walk with high heels on. Sexy is when you're confident and secure. Sexy is when you know what you want and how to get it. Sexy is when you look at someone with a fiery passion that is stronger and more moving than a touch could be, when a look can seduce you.

Sexy doesn't have to be loud. It can be very quiet. A look can say what words couldn't even repeat. A look can dominate you and bring you to your knees. A look can conquer your heart.

That's why they call it a temptation. It's something that you really want, that you can't resist. You rub the back of your neck and little beads of sweat start to form on your forehead. You imagine it in your mind as your heart starts to beat overtime. You're at a loss for words. You gulp down, take a breath, lick your lips...and eat that piece of chocolate cake!

There is nothing like chocolate! Chocolate is creamy and indulgent. Chocolate actually raises your level of endorphins! Chocolate can calm you down. It's downright tempting, that's what it is. Go ahead and have a chocolate moment!

I release and unleash my passion and love today! Watch out! Some dangerous things might happen. Lots of smiles, laughter and bliss may find you. You may get struck with love and give somebody the kiss of their life. Sexy might just take over the world.

When we feel powerful and sexy, others can feel it! You can knock people over with true confidence. Allow yourself to be passionate and feel things. Let people see that you have feelings and that you are not afraid to show them!

Calling all men! I say stand up and face the day with the kind of brilliance that is rooted in the strength that comes from being a real man. Walk past women today and remind us why we need you and can't live without you. Help us to recognize why we yearn so badly to take care of you and to be next to you. Show us again why we have followed you to the ends of the Earth.

I don't like the negative images of men because there are so many of you who are great role models. For some reason the world seems to praise the bad boy image. We need men to be strong but not mean and unkind. We need men to be great fathers and husbands. We need you.

POETRY TO MY LOVE

"HE LOVES ME, HE LOVES ME, HE REALLY LOVES ME...IN IMAGINING AND PICTURING THE LOVE OF MY LIFE, ONE IMPORTANT INGREDIENT WAS ALWAYS HIS EXCITEMENT FOR ME, TOO. LOVE IS A TWO-WAY STREET. I KNEW THAT I WOULD RECOGNIZE HIM AND WITHIN THAT RECOGNITION WOULD BE HIS EQUAL PASSION AND COMMITMENT TO ME.

I DON'T KNOW HOW TO DREAM WITHOUT YOU. WHEN I DREAM, YOU'RE ALWAYS THERE..."

I will be your muse. I will inspire you. I will be your joy, your love and your heart. I will shine for you like the sun. I will romance you like the light of the moon, and I will be your star. When you see darkness, seek me. I will shine brilliantly for you. I am your diamond, I will be your beauty, my lord. Not the kind of beauty that fades, but the beauty that renews from day to day. I will wake up like the morning sun to give you power. I will be your tenderness. Like a light drizzle of rain, I will refresh and soothe you. I will bring you peace. Your trust shall lay on my neck and your name at the tip of my lips. Ah my lord, I am yours.

I was aroused and attentive to the way Sarah referred to Abraham as her lord. I've used that expression as a sign of the deepest respect because that is why I think Sarah referred to him this way. As a teen, I became immersed in the poetic words belonging to "The Song Of Solomon." They enlivened me and stirred up my appetite for the highest quality of romance. Those words shaped my poetry, even my heart. This is when my poetry was born and my love ignited. My love is so ardent and devoted. Like a full-bodied red wine, my love is at the highest of content. It is unrelenting within my soul and consumes me, yet it is kind and tender. I can be fierce and sensual with it. Then, I can display the sincerity and gentleness of a child in need of its closeness. I am fervently obedient to love; I am love's trustworthy and steadfast servant. I love arduously with full intent and purpose.

I'll look at you dangerously. Don't underestimate my power. I am highly flammable, my lord. When I kiss you my sincerity will knock you over. Can I really be that excited and passionate? Yes, I promise you! I shall not ask for your heart, I will take it! You are superior to me in strength and so you laugh at the thought. But I will take you down like David took down Goliath. I have a little heart but when it hits you, you will fall and ask me for mercy. I will not give it to you; I will give you no mercy. I am the taker, and you are my goods—mine. Please bring your storm to me, your power. I am not afraid of lightning. I am not afraid of you.

I've always been attracted to a very strong male but that doesn't hinder or cast a shadow on my strength. I'm not afraid of the tallest and strongest of men. It's like a well-coordinated dance. I like to be pursued with power and I like to give it right back. When a man has that kind of might in him, it makes me feel comfortable, it puts me at ease. I yearn for a man with a commanding presence that can take charge in a respectful and peaceful manner. I like when a man is confident enough to let me strut my stuff, too.

Kiss me with the kisses of honey. Bathe me in love. Let your touch be soft and beautiful, like a dove. Let your eyes touch every part of me. May your lips be soft and may they impart sweetness upon me. May you mark me with your scent, my dear one. May you set me aside as belonging to you. I do long for you. You will be known in the gates, because of the way I speak of you. You will be spoken about because of the way I am taken by you. You command an army, my love, and that is me. I am your army. I am your queen.

How can a man accomplish great things if his own wife doesn't believe in him? Believing in the man in my life is essential. I will exalt and venerate him at home and in public, as he will adore and respect me. A relationship is the best of partnerships. You should always try to make your other half look better. You build up your home, as Proverbs says. You do not tear it down. It is important for a woman to not only let a man be a man but to support him in his manhood. I will stroke his ego with honesty and willingness.

Perhaps he will come and throw me over his back and take me one day. I like the sound of that. But he will know that I command many and that I am tall in spirit! He will look to me for help; I will have amity with him. He will recognize my strength and he will adhere to it because a warrior respects a true warrior and I am one. I will match the strength of his arm with the strength of

my heart. My bow and arrow is as fast as his sword. My dear one is away in the battle and so I care for things. I can fight and protect what is mine. I can get along without him. In his absence, I take his place and protect what is his and that is me and all of me. Loyalty is a must, as I am his empire. He is mine, I desire no other. That is how I have been made.

I will stand beside him and fight through life with him. I will also enjoy peace with him. I want us to be partners and encourage each other. So, in my own way, I will be a warrior, too. I will go out to the war with him and conquer beside him. We will both be powerful in our own ways. I believe in respecting a man's strength. I am not the kind of woman who will tell my man what to do. He is my king, I am his queen, make no mistake about that. It is a union, a respectful alliance of hearts.

He is quite the warrior. He could stand against anyone and his sword would claim the victory. He is formidable in heart and in the heat of battle, he is someone to watch. He is a leader and I have so much admiration for him. I show him a great deal of respect. The strength in his eyes matches the passion in mine. His touch startles my heart and takes movement in me.

My passion and love are explosive! My loyalty is unyielding and my journey for the man I want is worth it. I see men that I admire and that is a necessary ingredient in the love I will have for my mate. I am taken by him and just the thought of him startles and moves my heart. I am so sure of him that when I come back to read this section of my book, I will be wowed at how well my poetry captures him. He has been put in my heart and every day of my life I have been brought closer and closer to him.

The thunder of your heart beckons me. The smolder of my desire for you is the sweetest pain. I am a fire my lord, I will not ask for mercy. I will break into your arms. I will approach the lion within you with no fear. I will match the strength of your soul. I will look into your eyes without turning away. I will release my city of gold to you in a kiss and leave with your heart as my spoil from war. I will do this all before I surrender to you.

I am a fighter but when it comes down to it, I will surrender to my man. I don't surrender but to the man in my life, I will be gentle and let him see my heart. Before I wave my white flag, I will conquer him! I will knock him over with a heart full of spirit and a deep soul. I will drench him in my honesty, my excitement and my depth.

I don't love the perfection of you. It wasn't the success of you that grabbed me. It was the good that I saw you do, it was your heart. Your heart was even bigger than your body. So, I want the depths of you. You can share your fears, even your tears, with me, although I know you're so strong. You have no idea what you have in me. If you have me, you have a good thing, indeed. If you were the richest man in the world, you couldn't buy me and not even the richest man in the world could take me away from you. I love you.

I know that he has a big heart. I know that his big heart is even bigger than his commanding presence! I see power, strength and a lot of heart! There is nothing better than a man who is strong, very manly, and still tender. No man is a wall and I want to see his weaknesses. What he hides from others, I want him to share his soul with me. When I become his, I will be a great strength to him and no other man will be able to take me from him. He is my forever and my always.

I am loyal like the earth is to the rain. I will stay faithful to you like the sun is to the day. I am waiting to write your name on my heart. I am anxious to play you the song on my lips, to release, to unleash my spirit onto you. I want all of you. Yes, you are awesome, I know.

My dear one will recognize my voice, my hands, my lips, even the way I stand. I am so sure of this that my heart is patient and protected. Nothing could break it, it can only get distracted. Only the right man can take it. We attract that person into our lives at the right time. When you do attract that person, you recognize each other. It is the soul's recognition of its match. It's almost something familiar but so surprising at the same time. You just know, and I believe he will be just as sure about me as I am about him.

It's a feeling. I sense it. I feel you. It's as if you know when someone approaches me. Your jealousy touches my spirit. I am bound to you. Others come for me, but I cannot turn to them. I only want you. I breathe your air. Sometimes when I close my eyes, I can almost see you. It feels like rushing waters, a stampede of horses running through my heart. Then, all the sudden, I am in a peaceful garden of roses. The warmth of the sun touches my thigh. I beg of the day not to wake my body from this blissful sleep. Please don't go, and let no one awaken me.

I don't believe that I have the right to just give myself to anyone. I belong to the love of my life and that is powerful. I treat love and romance as special. Since it is special, then I don't just give it out to anyone. I will be romanced for the last time and I feel that coming. It makes me have a formidable patience. I have a prince, I have a king. There is no reason for me to entertain an imposter. So, I walk in the protection he gives me, now.

Silence speaks no words, a touch moves throughout my spirit. It's so powerful I almost feel a rush of tears. I gasp for breath as my heart skips a beat. I lay back my head, as your chest magnetically moves to the response of mine. You put me in a willing submission. And it was just a kiss.

O' but it is so sweet. I have prepared for it. The waiting makes it better. I can't replay it, O' but I can. It's the simple things, when the simple things can make your day. One kiss, no, one kiss from the right person will set you in bliss.

I can count on him. I can call to him. He can melt me like ice cream in the hot summer sun. He holds me like the stream holds a rock in its gentle embrace. He is someone who can carry me. He is full of charm and I like it. He is powerful like an eagle in flight and becomes a dove in my sight. He is a man, and I love him more than chocolate cake, and I love chocolate cake.

It is no secret to my friends that I love chocolate, and so does my son! I tell people, when he was a baby, I knew he was mine because he was crazy for chocolate just like his mommy! To say I love my man more than chocolate cake, now that is love!

I am a black stallion. If you try to contain me, I will throw you down like a cowboy who needs to be taught a lesson.

I have fire that you cannot control. The one who will brand me is the one I belong to. I will respond to his voice. If you're not my owner, you will know it! I will reject you with a force you cannot stand against. Don't try to saddle me. Don't try to rein me in. Don't put a fence around me. I don't give in, only to him, yes, only to him. I am tame with him, but only before I run free again. No fences for me, but I willingly stay in his stable of protection.

I've always been enchanted with black stallions. They are lovely and magnificent, they fascinate me. I relate to their power. I like a free stallion running wild, which is what I feel is the spirit I capture at times. This is why there are some that get frustrated with me because there is no taming me. I've had guys try to outsmart me or get me to let them lead me. It doesn't work for them. I will only follow the lead of one man, the one that is for me. Those that have tried to take that position have found out really quickly that it belongs to one and no one else.

I am not a beggar my lord, nor am I impoverished. I am rich in spirit; I am bountiful in love and generous at heart. I am not a passenger, I am a driver. I will dwell in your dominion, in your great power, in your awesome strength and I shall give you mine. But I am not a beggar my lord, so if you are not mine, you may freely go. I am not in need, I am in want. I don't need a hostage, I want a king. I want you.

This has always been one of my favorite poems. I feel so deeply and my love for him will be overwhelming but he must meet me with the same intensity. I am not looking for a prisoner of love; I am looking for my love, my king! If he would want to go, he could go freely because the man for me is not a hostage, he is my partner and recognizes his need for me.

I will wait for you, even forever. I will awaken like the morning, but it is still night. And no one can awaken me but you. I'll kiss you like you've never been kissed before. I will breathe my life into you. In one breathless, desperate moment, I will put my arms around you, close my eyes and let you see my wild horses, my love, my frenzy, my vulnerability, my playful fury, my innocent frustration, my peaceful fire. I will look into your eyes and you will see me relish in my craving for you and you will feast on that rush!

Everything I do is filled with feeling. I can kiss with all my heart! I am very affectionate and I am not ashamed or afraid to show it. That is one of the best parts of me. I can communicate through feeling, looking, or touching. I can say without saying.

You awakened the music in me. Like violins your eyes played the strings of my soul ever so gently. Did you read my notes or did you just know my song? You made my heart beat like a drum. Like a piano you hit the high note with me and my breath became an instrument to your kiss. As my conductor, your hands lead the orchestra of me to play a beautiful song.

I liken love and romance to the beauty of music. When two hearts beat together, it can make a special ballad. Two people in love can write a melody that is only played when they are together. When two souls become one, it is like hearing an orchestra play in perfect tune and togetherness.

Yes I am known in the village, they send the young women to me, I teach them. I am the mother of many and you are in the battle. I wait for you; I care for your wounds. I live in your hut. I pray for you. God knows He must bring you back to me, or I would stop breathing. My survival is your survival. I need you, as you need me.

When I say that he is away at war, I am saying that he is a man that is busy doing good things. He is trying to make a difference in this world and I support him in that. I care for his wounds when he does come home to me. I pray for him because he is involved in so much and needs support. He needs healing and I am the one to help heal his wounds. I will bandage him up with my tenderness and my love so that he can go back out and fight the world again and again. He can count on my support.

Hold me like you will be the last to touch me. I want to come home. I want to land in a nest that can hold me and warm my soul. I want to fly away and always come back to you. Make me a magnet to you. Look at me with eyes consumed with jealousy over me.

My man will claim me. He will be my nest, my home. I will be able to fly away into life and do all that I enjoy doing. I will go out in the world and try to make a difference everyday and come home to him. That is what life is all about, having a home. I want him to be my home, his arms, his eyes and his soul.

Take me over, make me still. You rescue me and I'll rescue you. Pin me down and I'll pin you. You wrestle me and I'll wrestle you! Let's play a game of heart tag, can I be it?

I am very playful and I always want to have fun with my partner. I like to wrestle, and I may not win, but I still like to try. Couples that play together, stay together.

Who could capture my spirit? It's like trying to catch the wind but you caught me. You're a doorway to keep me safe. Your arms protect me from the rain. I'm like a waterfall and you are my ocean, so I pour into you. I'm a fire that cannot be contained and you're my fireplace.

I get lost in his greatness and that holds me and calms me. I am a fire and so in some way, he equals me but also defuses me, in a good way. It's always good for couples to strike a balance. A good relationship juggles the differences in it well.

I have taken off my coat. How can I put it back on? I am by the fire, so warm and so comfortable. My eyes reflect the flames and I am quiet, I am content. I am a fire, my love, to keep you warm, to keep you warm. How can a fire be so peaceful? I don't know, but I am peaceful.

My best moments are when I am passionate, yet very peaceful. I can have a clear mind and heart and experience peace, yet I can feel the fire in my soul. My fire can turn into a flame on a candle so that I can be held.

I could write a book about the peace I feel in your arms. In your arms, every time I was wounded, is taken away. In your arms, every time I was alone, is gone from my memory completely. In your arms, nothing can touch me or harm me. In your arms, I am safe. I could write a book about the way I feel in your arms.

Sometimes I want to rest in arms bigger than mine. Sometimes I want to take the weights on my shoulders and lay them down. But I always want to be the tiger I am, the bull in spirit, and the woman of faith that I am. Saying all that, I have to admit that in your arms, I feel safe. In your arms, I don't have to bark. You take my big bark down to that of a poodle. In your arms I'm small. I like the way that feels but then again, I'm still Miss Big stuff! But I like your arms.

Make no mistake about it, you are mine. They can look, they can smile, but you are mine to touch. If you need me, believe me, I will rise up and they will know I am coming. I am a queen, yes, yes I am.

Every woman has to know her unique quality, her beauty that is only hers. A woman has to know that when a man loves her, there is no other woman for him. I know that what is mine is mine. There is no woman who can be me. No woman can smile like me or be sexy like me, so my man is captured by his love for me. When a man loves a woman, that is his woman and no one else compares to her.

I humbly acknowledge my dependency on you, needing you sometimes. You are my compass, without you I lack some type of direction. I submit to you, and your leadership I long for patiently. I admire you and my admiration is not easy to come by. As I sit on my throne and rule my own kingdom as I daily walk into the world as the lioness I am, I remember you. You wear a crown and I decorate it with honor. I bow to no one but I rise to you.

I am an independent woman in the sense that I can make it. I think that sometimes this independent woman movement is taken too far. I am independent but I need the man in my life. There is nothing wrong with a woman letting a man know that she needs him, that he is the one for her. There is nothing wrong with a woman letting him know, that she admires him and looks up to him. Just as a man needs his woman, a woman needs her man.

When you told me I was beautiful I believed it. I knew that I must be; that it had to be true. Your eyes and lips told me so. The way you touched me sealed every word. You make me feel like I'm the only woman in the world. You make me feel like the example of what a woman should be. The way you look at me would make Eve jealous and cause Adam to turn his head. Somehow you made me more desirable. You make me smile just by existing.

Before you even knew me, I was blessed with the fact that you existed. You see, just because I know you're alive, I'm happy. Meeting and knowing a man who can completely take my breath away and make all my poetry come true is beyond me. Before you even said hello to me, everyday you blessed my existence with yours. I didn't know it was possible to love someone all your life before even meeting them, but I met that possibility when I met you. I've never been moved like this or kissed the way you kiss me.

MY SPIRIT

"I AM A QUEEN. I SIT IN CONFIDENCE AND PEACE. WANT HAS LEFT ME AND HAVING HAS REPLACED IT WITH PEACE. FEAR HAS FLOWN FROM MY NEST. FAITH AND WISDOM HAVE RECLAIMED ME. I LIVE WITH HEART AND SOUL. LOVE GIVES ME POWER SO NO ONE CAN OVERTHROW ME. I AM PROTECTED BY LOVE. GOD IS LOVE, AND I FEEL LOVE."

I looked deep into the handsome eyes of excitement today. I embraced positive; fulfillment dipped me back and gave me a big kiss. Productive has claimed me. Amazing told me that I belonged to great things. Impossible and miracle are fighting over me, and I admit that I've been flirting with happiness. I grabbed joy and gave my heart to possibilities. I am so in love with this day. I will do some great things today!

I have a blissful spirit and I awaken with adoration for the day! I seize the day with attentiveness and focus on the treasure of each moment that I live in.

I have been blindfolded with blessings and joy has locked me up with goodness. I guess I'm a willing prisoner. I'm just going to be forced to smile and have good experiences today. I can't help it, I just can't help it. I'm biting my lip and my cheeks are blushing, my smile is so full of liveliness that my eyes are sparkling. I've

looked into the face of obstacle today and changed its name to possibilities! I said, "Bring it on," because I have been dipped in success. Blessings await me.

I walk with joy daily and I get drunk with happiness. Now that is what living is. I have really fallen in love with life and all the wonderful daily possibilities, miracles and blessings that I encounter. It's like I'm trying to explain to you the most beautiful thing I've ever seen. But how can I explain the beauty of falling in love with life? I am thankful that God led me to this place. You have to feel it yourself and you will know exactly what I am talking about.

I was heavily meditating on something and all of a sudden a familiar face showed up beside me. I took off my headset and started talking to my friend. On the way, I saw another friend I needed to smile and say hello to. I was quickly reminded that today wasn't about me. Today is about reaching out to others and answering my calling to care, listen and share.

I was in prayer to God about something that was troubling me. It was so important that it consumed me on my walk to work. I was listening to a gospel song that was stressing the need to be patient and wait on God. I had enjoyed my weekend but my concern was still on my mind on Monday. So, those two familiar faces showing up on my way to work was God's answer to my prayer. The answer was to help others and to think about them. That has always been God's answer in my life. I am best when I am helping others, I was made for it and my heart has a deep and overwhelming capacity to love. Caring for others is like a need to me. I was made for it, and I want to do it.

When I was a teenager, I used to pray to God to take away my want to ever get married. I decided that I would be a much better minister that way. I kept realizing that instead of a decrease, I was becoming completely and absolutely passionate! I asked God to take it away, but it didn't happen. That's when I started writing poetry about my dear one. So, God says 'No' sometimes, at least to me! But most of the time he says 'Yes,' or God tells me, *I'm going to do that but much better than you could ask or even imagine.* Perhaps that is why he didn't let that feeling go away. It could have been because the fulfillment of it would be even better!

When I was growing up, I remember going out in the ministry since I could walk! I met this really nice older man who told me a story that I've never forgotten. He said he wanted to be a priest but as soon as he saw a woman in a skirt, he changed his mind! I went back to see him as much as I could. I would share a scripture with him and he would listen. One time when I went back to see him, his wife was there and she told me he had died. That broke my heart.

What he said stayed with me and I would agree with him, just not about the skirt part. I've got passion, and I think God made me that way on purpose for a purpose.

Be careful how close you stand to me just for a moment until my passion subsides. The electricity that is flowing from my soul right now could light up a city...Slow down heart, slow down soul. You need not conquer the world in a day. Slow down passion, intensity and bliss. You'll set a forest on fire like this. Slow down tigress, it's only the morning! Let the lioness of you rest. In peace, I am

calm. Peace brings my soul into submission. In peace, I am silent for a moment.

If it were not for my smile, my power would overwhelm you. When you really see my strength in spirit, you will wonder how I stay contained, how I'm so peaceful. You will think this mild in comparison and you will know why sometimes I just get so intense and passionate. I bubble over like champagne! But I can still be very peaceful and caring. The peace always comes to calm me down and I have balance.

My honesty, you love me for my honesty. That is a good thing, because I like being honest. You have embraced my inner beauty and that makes me feel more beautiful than I thought possible. Thank you for letting me be me.

I say how I truly feel and I am happy people like me for that. The closest thing to reality I have is how I feel about everything. It may not always be the truth, but it is how I feel, so it is true to me. I like when I walk in that. I don't like to hide behind anything. There is nothing like a truthful word, a truthful smile, or a truthful kiss. Try it sometime. Just be in the moment, the kiss of life.

See the beauty in me now while I am climbing. While I am weak, embrace me. Love me now when I don't do all the things you think I should. Love me the way I am and the way I want to be. Don't wait for me to be perfect because you just might miss me. If I could be your perfect, I would be, but I can only be perfectly me.

I recommend for everyone to love the people in your life throughout the journey they are on, not when they reach the destination.

For those of you who can't hang, I don't know what to say to you. To those of you who are with me, let's love and care for those who need help. Let's love and care for those who need some warriors to come in and save them. Let's look after widows, fatherless boys, the weak, the humble and the poor. Let's be the conquerors we are. Let us take out our love and stand for those who cannot stand for themselves.

My goal is to do my best to help others. How can we just look the other way? We have to see people and help those in need. The world needs more compassion.

There are times when vulnerability exposes the fragile place that dwells within me. I am a bull in spirit and full of heart. I can rise up with faith and be the fierce queen that I am. I can turn into the fighting lioness of me in an instant and the warrior of me is not afraid of the battle life throws before me. Still, sometimes I am the unsure little girl of me, who is jumping into God's arms looking for protection and I get it!

Vulnerability can be a great strength. It can feel a little scary at times. Opening yourself up can be a challenge. Try to do something you have failed at before. Expose yourself to public opinion, hurt, heartache, and even embarrassment. My greatest strength is always in my weakest moments. When I am brave enough to be weak in front of you or just to be weak, I am my strongest. My faith is shown in weakness.

I'm thankful that God saw my potential. You may not see your gifts and our society may not see your beauty. Your family may reject you, but there is always someone who loves you and believes in you. That includes me. I know you can do it because somehow I turned out alright. Man sometimes trashes what God treasures most, people!

I really do love the people in my life and there are many. They all have stories and I see the light and beauty in them.

There is no convincing me. If my heart is not inclined, then my heart is not inclined. I am loyal and so passionate that when my heart is shaken, it is like an earthquake that could take out a village with an aftershock that could awaken the moon and make it call for the day. When I close my door, it cannot be broken into. If I am not inclined, there is no convincing me...unmovable.

When I was a child, I wasn't a follower. If someone tried to make me go right, I would go left. Whatever I did, it was out of a willing spirit and because I thought about it. I have not changed. I am not obedient; I am willing. I decide and I can defend myself like you can't even imagine. I can be just like that snot-nosed little girl I was, and if I don't want you in the swing next to me, well then, you can't sit there. You can't make me do anything, but why would you want to?

I'd recommend having a tiger as a pet, feeding a lion, taming a stallion, bull fighting, sky diving, having a picnic on the 33 of JanuFeb and bringing Tina and Ike back together before you try to make me do anything. Some things in life are just not meant to be controlled, and I'm one of them.

Just watch me. Watch me conquer. Watch me fly. I am rising, my wings are soaring. There is no sharp shooter who can take me down. No storm that scares me away from the sky. Thunder hears me coming and the rain knows me. Yes, I have been rained on many times. There

is not a hunter that can get close enough, and I have faith as my wind. Strength is my guide, so watch me! Watch me fly.

I can't help but smile in the rain. We all make choices. I made mine. I never did the gold digger thing. I didn't sit up under my momma; I chose to run out in the rain. I wasn't afraid. I'm still not. I feel beautiful because of my trials, making it through the pain of a heart broken and crushed, carrying my son without a man to hold my hand, I'm still standing. Come on storm, come get me. I know how to fly.

I am a fire, a fire that cannot be put out. I am a rose, a rose that cannot be uprooted. I am a diamond, a diamond that cannot be bought. Priceless. You cannot contain me. I have figured out my power and now, there is no stopping me. I am a butterfly that cannot be caught. There isn't a net that can hold me.

I used to have haters. That makes me laugh now. Once I started to really stand in my strength, no one could stand against me. Being kind made me put up with so much. Now, I don't even except foolishness for a minute, and then I give that look like, 'Yes, you just ran across one of the baddest females around.' I am the lioness! I'm still kind; I just walk in my power!

I am a bull in spirit. I'm stubborn, impatient, wise, peaceful and a brat at times. I am as sweet as can be. I can be like honey or like a strong drink with no ice. I can be a kiss or a kick in the butt. I can be a mommy, a diva, and you better believe a human being. I am very human, a spicy little thing I am.

You have got to like or love me for me, and whenever I look around at a party for me, I am going to know the people in the room. My life is going to be full and meaningful, always. My marriage will be real, my career will be real. My life will always reflect the beauty of authenticity! I will be me and you can count on that!

Caramel, yep, that's me. Sugar, I've got that, too. Better yet, brown sugar, butterscotch and milk chocolate chips, a gentle touch, a come and get me look, but just for that one guy, a cup of passion, a dash of self-control, peace, bake me in peace...Instead of water, pour in some love...Done!

My Granny used to call me honey pot and I am full of honey. Did somebody say pass the sugar? I make sure to pass on the sweetness of me daily. Every time I walk by someone, I wish them well in my spirit and I give off the positive energy that saturates me. I say to pass some sweetness of your own today. May the recipe of you be filled with so much love that you leave someone a sweet tooth. The more you pass, the more that comes back to you.

Nobody can be me like I can. Nobody can go from talking about sports to getting their nails done better than I can! Nobody can be as stubborn as me and change so very quickly. Nobody can be as honest about the way I feel or more proud of the way I live. Nobody smiles like me or wears high heels quite like me.

I look back at the good. I look forward to the good. No regrets, just growth. I step into my future, without fear. There is a place for me. It feels good to know who I am and to have my own identity. Aside from religion, a relationship, being a mother, or my work, I am me. I have stepped beyond those things. I walk in my own shoes and they're kind of sexy!

I'm no longer a caged bird, so there's no need to catch me. When I take refuge in my tree of protection, stop thinking you can get me. I can fly, I can soar. I'm a smart little bird. I will surprise you with my flight! You cannot contain me. I belong to no one. I am not a caged bird. I am free.

I regained that fearless child I once was. I found that little girl that played kick ball with the boys in the neighborhood, that little tough girl that watched *The Godfather* and football with my Dad. That same girl who went to church with my Mom and talked politics and religion with my friends' parents. Back then, I thought I needed to be different when I was perfect the way I was.

I remember walking to school and praying the whole way there. I remember talking and walking with God, and when I was scared he made me strong. I asked God for wisdom nightly and he gave my heart wings to fly.

I remember being little and afraid. I remember hearing my parents fighting and praying throughout the night because I couldn't sleep. I remember going to school and being different because of what I struggled with at home. My self-esteem wasn't built up and I didn't know how to fit in or be normal, if there even is a normal. I had no idea that people found me attractive and that seemed to alienate me more. I just wanted to be liked and have friends. I felt lonely and in that loneliness God listened to me and became my best friend. God gave me courage and helped me find my beauty and strength.

Sometimes I act like I'm taller than I really am. I remember when I was in school and I was taller than the guys. There was even a time I was just as strong as they were. Then, they got taller and stronger. I have the heart of a lioness, but I'm realizing, I'm kind of like a girl. I think I'm a linebacker but I'm really just a shorty…

Growing up in a family that valued men so much didn't help me learn how to be a girl. Thankfully, I am so naturally a girly girl in so many ways, I can't help it. I always wanted to run with the boys, though, and do the things they could do. I came from a family of strong men and I wanted to be strong, too. I learned this really macho attitude that is still with me today. I would stand toe-to-toe with anyone and not back down regardless of the fact that I'm 5' 8" and not that big. I think I got into a few fights that way. I also protected and stood up and fought for many with my big bark. God gave me a monstrous spirit. The wildest thing about all that is I can still look up at you with this big sincere smile, blush at you and show you that the girl in me is just hiding sometimes, but she's always there.

I have earned my stripes. I look like a flower but I have a heart of steel. Looking at me, you would never know where I have been. I have come from a struggle. That is why I reach out to help. I have been prepared for my throne and so I sit. Don't be fooled, there is a giant under my smile. I am a lioness and I will rise to the challenge! I always do.

People tell me often that I have surprised them. Many expect me to be a certain way but I am not what they expect. I have always been down to earth. Life has taken me in places and changed me for the good. I don't admire people because of the way they look or how much money they have. Social status doesn't impress me. I have friends from all different backgrounds and places. I look at the man sitting outside my building begging for food as just as important as the president of a company, or a celebrity. I care and it's so important to me that I communicate that. I try to look in the eyes of all with the kind of love and respect I want to be given.

I didn't know my great power before but now I do. That man is in trouble, I promise you. I am a linebacker, fast, strong and smooth. He can't get past me; I've got all the winning moves. Going in for the tackle and I'll sack him, too! And that's not all, O' no, that's not all!

I am something alright! I have a way of saying things and doing things that is unique to me. I remember when my Granny told me how she met my Grandfather. She said he asked her to wrestle and before she knew it she was pregnant. Well, I decided then that I would challenge the man I would be with to wrestle. I wanted to win then and I still do. I'm thinking he will be able to take me but it's the thought that counts, and I think I can take him down. I promise you this: I will try to with all my might!

Don't check me unless you can check me. Let me say that again. Don't check me unless you can check me. Let me say that again. Don't come into the den of the lioness if you don't know how to calm me, or if you look like a piece of steak. Come in peace or come for a discussion.

You can disagree with me or even be disagreeable. But if you must try to check me, make sure you are up to the task.

I am not disagreeable, I just don't always agree. I'm done trying to play the, "I'm so nice and I'm not going to tell it to you like it is" role. Now, I don't challenge to challenge and I don't argue or insist on my way. I think about what I say. I say what I mean and mean what I say. I have an educated opinion and I don't mind sharing it. I say exactly what is on my mind most of the time so take it or leave it. If you want to challenge me, then be up to the task of doing that. I'm not speaking out to hear my own voice. I say everything from a place because I feel and think. I ask that people respect that about me and know that when you challenge me, I can take the challenge, but can you?

I possess many colors. I am not perfect; I am simply, perfectly me.

I have come to love myself and appreciate who I am, and I recommend this for everyone. You have a treasure and that is you. It isn't so important to me that I show you my best side. It's more important to me that I show you who I really am, flaws and all! That is the beauty of life. It isn't in the perfection I show you, it's my individuality that will make you look at me. I'd rather you like me for who I am.

I can tell a woman how beautiful she is because her beauty does not diminish mine. It encourages me and uplifts me to see truly talented and beautiful women everywhere, all around the world! I can't take credit for how I was born, but I can take some credit for how I try to live. I want people to see the beauty in the way I live.

I recognize my authenticity and my uniqueness. I am a whole person and the outside of me is a part of me, it's just a part. I like the entire me; I like what I hope I bring to your mind when you see me. I hope I make you smile when you read what I've been able to write. When I am able to show kindness, or when I have the privilege to help or give, those are the times I feel most attractive. I am proud of myself when you are proud of me. I hope you think of my sense of humor and my willingness to say how I feel. When you think of me, don't forget that I am a tiger but still a gentle flower. I love hard, and that is the best part of me. When I step outside of myself and think of others, I feel so pretty. When my eyes sparkle because I am thankful, I feel it and that feeling is better than someone telling me that my shoes look nice. When I can feel my cheeks blush because I'm so happy, I think I must look my best in that moment.

Tenderness wraps around my consciousness and I find myself quieting down. Instead of a fire, I simmer with gentle warmth that caresses my inner struggle. My heart postulates that I surrender to its calling for a steadfast eagerness in all that I do. The intensity that resides in my eyes has made a covenant with my heart to chastise my soul's craving for peace. So I find refuge in my obedience to tenderness.

It's so important to be productive and persistent. I like to stay busy but sometimes I need to rest. The truth is I don't do that so easily, I struggle with it. I find rest in being passionately tender at times, it's a compromise. I pride myself at being good in all that I do. I direct eagerness into meditating on kindness and tenderness. We all must find balance and this is how I find mine.

The real test is growing in wisdom while remaining humble. Move on to the glorious with innocence and love. Get to that next level and still pray like you have your last dollar.

Don't let this world make you fit into it or drown you of your ability to trust, to care, or to reach out. I feel my naivety leaving me but it's the best part of me. I don't want to stop being that excited little girl who got up in the morning ready to go to Disney World. I like the part of me that believes the best and that when I fall in love it will be forever. I always want to love hard and true. The fact that I can do that is a gift. No matter what I get or how much I know, I still want to live each day with newness.

Being a bad chick now is actually being able to read a book, cook, be a momma and go to work! I'm a new kind of bad chick! I don't have to get an attitude, or talk all loud and role my neck. Instead I've got what it takes to act like I've got some sense, now that is my kind of bad.

It's not original anymore to have an attitude. It's not authentic anymore to be the woman who can fight. I am a strong woman because I can be kind. I know how to keep a home and I love my family. I will always stand up and protect those that are mine. I would stand up to protect anyone that I could and that makes me proud of myself. I'm not going to try to run the streets and act tough. I am tough because I have integrity and I walk in love. I am trustworthy and I am there working hard from day to day. I try to help people and that is how I show that I am strong.

Take the great leap of faith and start enjoying your life. You don't know what's coming next but you take the first jump anyway. The bigger you jump, the bigger the arms are that catch you. I risk myself so that I may truly live up to my full potential. I test myself to the ultimate limits and each time I find that I have no limits. I'm a cat on a hot tin roof and I always land on my feet.

I risk myself because you're worth it. I know that if you're reading this book that it's for a reason. You are ready to take life to the next level, and I want you to. I want you to know that you are the miracle you've been waiting for. You are just as unique and amazing as anyone that you see walking around this Earth. I am extraordinary and so are you. Your job in life is to discover that.

I don't want you to imprison yourself any longer. Take the limits off your mind. Rewrite your life to reflect beauty and joy in every way. Push everything into the light and into the positive. Get out a mental pen and start rewriting life the way you want it to be, and don't be afraid of disappointment. Believe and have faith that good things are bound to happen to you.

Use your creative power to make the world better today. Do whatever you do to heal others and the world. That is powerful; you are powerful.

The joy you've been waiting for is something you can connect to whenever you choose to. You are extraordinary and you can do anything you want to. Believe in you, because you wouldn't be here if you were not special. Everyone living is special. You were made on purpose for a great and wonderful purpose. Walk in it, my friend!

ABOUT THE AUTHOR

Chicago's Finest: Juana Wooldridge

BIO

Capable and committed, Juana Wooldridge holds the power to become a character and make the audience believe. Her passion for life has taken her from her home in California to Chicago. Competitive by nature, she competed on the Speech and Debate Team at Harper College in Illinois. Her powerful command of language and reason gives her an edge as an actress. Her ability to surrender to the character and become someone else has given her a greater understanding of the human condition and a compassion for people that surpasses many strong women. Wise beyond her years, she brings understanding to characters and makes them come alive. Cast in a lead role for a series, Juana Wooldridge has just begun a meteoric rise. She sings, she dances and she commands. Soon everyone will know her name.

As a writer, Juana Wooldridge brings architecture of words that delight the spirit. Her need to express and her need to share bring a beauty to others as she weaves the tapestry of her thoughts into words that linger in hearts and minds.

A motivational speaker, Juana Wooldridge enchants her audiences with her own strength of character. She brings hope, inspiration and challenge to audiences. She dares them to be more than expected as she shares her story. She is a single mother with the drive to win against all odds. She encourages, cajoles, and sometimes scolds as she takes the audience on a journey to self-awareness.

Juana Wooldridge gives back. Her compassion and her sense of duty make her commit to helping others. Treasured memories of family set her feet on a path to help others. Her need to excel is matched by a need to serve her community. Juana Wooldridge is the voice of hope to people struggling and the voice of comfort to those discouraged. Juana Wooldridge is their angel. – Written by Sheryl Dolley

ABOUT THE EDITOR - Leslie Gordon

Bio

Leslie Gordon is an entertainment journalist, published writer and editor who breathes life into memoirs, feature stories, celebrity interviews, creative briefs and press materials. She is a speechwriter for the Magic Johnson Foundation and her writing experience ranges from business communiqués to magazine features, from social commentary to short stories, from public relations plans to advertising copy, from restaurant reviews to poetry. In 2009, she became a contributing author of the NAACP award-nominated anthology entitled *Family Affair: What it Means to be African American Today* (Agate/Bolden).

Leslie has been called a rainmaker, a strategist, an idea generator and a communications and marketing thought leader. She is one of the creative forces behind myriad successful public relations and marketing campaigns – from Walt Disney World's Disney Dreamers Academy to Daddy's Promise, a national initiative designed to focus attention on the positive relationship that can and should exist between fathers and daughters. She earned a Bachelor of Science degree in advertising from the University of Illinois and a Master's degree in humanities from the University of Chicago.

Leslie is a marathon runner, and a Bikram yoga and Pilates enthusiast. She resides in West Bloomfield, Michigan with her three children and her husband, Emmy award-winning broadcast journalist, Ed Gordon.

"Juana what comes to my head when I think of you and your writing is: Sexy, breathtaking, heartfelt, unconditional love and powerful!"

~Toni Shelton, Los Angeles, California

How to book Juana for speaking engagements:
Juana Wooldridge
e-mail: juanajdub@gmail
blog: juanatalk.blogspot.com

220 Communications
phone: 1-866-533-9884
e-mail: info@220Communications.com